eLmL 2019

The Eleventh International Conference on Mobile, Hybrid, and On-line Learning

February 24 – 28, 2019

Athens, Greece

eLmL 2019 Editors

Herwig Mannaert, University of Antwerp, Belgium

Printed from e-media with permission by:

Curran Associates, Inc.
57 Morehouse Lane
Red Hook, NY 12571

Some format issues inherent in the e-media version may also appear in this print version.

Printed by Curran Associates, Inc. (2019)

International Academy, Research, and Industry Association (IARIA)
412 Derby Way
Wilmington, DE 19810

Phone: (408) 893-6407
Fax: (408) 527-6351

petre@iaria.org

Additional copies of this publication are available from:

Curran Associates, Inc.
57 Morehouse Lane
Red Hook, NY 12571 USA
Phone: 845-758-0400
Fax: 845-758-2633
Email: curran@proceedings.com
Web: www.proceedings.com

Table of Contents

eLmL 2019

Forward

The eleventh edition of the International Conference on Mobile, Hybrid, and On-line Learning (eLmL 2018), held in Athens, Greece, February 24 - 28, 2019, focused on the latest trends in e-learning and also on the latest IT technology alternatives that are poised to become mainstream strategies in the near future and will influence the e-learning environment.

eLearning refers to on-line learning delivered over the World Wide Web via the public Internet or the private, corporate intranet. The goal of the eLmL 2019 conference was to provide an overview of technologies, approaches, and trends that are happening right now. The constraints of e-learning are diminishing and options are increasing as the Web becomes increasingly easy to use and the technology becomes better and less expensive.

eLmL 2019 provided a forum where researchers were able to present recent research results and new research problems and directions related to them. The topics covered aspects related to tools and platforms, on-line learning, mobile learning, and hybrid learning.

We take this opportunity to thank all the members of the eLmL 2019 Technical Program Committee as well as the numerous reviewers. The creation of such a broad and high-quality conference program would not have been possible without their involvement. We also kindly thank all the authors who dedicated much of their time and efforts to contribute to the eLmL 2019. We truly believe that, thanks to all these efforts, the final conference program consists of top quality contributions.

This event could also not have been a reality without the support of many individuals, organizations, and sponsors. We are grateful to the members of the eLmL 2019 organizing committee for their help in handling the logistics and for their work to make this professional meeting a success.

We hope that eLmL 2019 was a successful international forum for the exchange of ideas and results between academia and industry and for the promotion of progress in eLearning research.

We also hope that Athens provided a pleasant environment during the conference and everyone saved some time for exploring this beautiful city.

eLmL 2019 Chairs

eLmL Steering Committee

Herwig Mannaert, University of Antwerp, Belgium
Stephen White, The University of Huddersfield - Queensgate, UK
Maiga Chang, Athabasca University, Canada
Hironori Washizaki, Waseda University, Japan
Krzysztof Szklanny, Polish-Japanese Academy of Information Technology, Poland
Christian M. Stracke, Open University of the Netherlands, The Netherlands
Ivan Ganchev, University of Limerick, Ireland / Plovdiv University "Paisii Hilendarski", Bulgaria
Tomayess Issa, Curtin University, Australia
Yifat Ben-David Kolikant, Hebrew University of Jerusalem, Israel
Mudasser Wyne, National University - San Diego, USA

eLmL Industry/Research Advisory Committee

Michael Verhaart, Eastern Institute of Technology Hawke's Bay, New Zealand
Guglielmo Trentin, Institute of Educational Technology of the Italian National Research Council (ITD-CNR), Italy

eLmL 2019

COMMITTEE

eLmL Steering Committee

Herwig Mannaert, University of Antwerp, Belgium
Stephen White, The University of Huddersfield - Queensgate, UK
Maiga Chang, Athabasca University, Canada
Hironori Washizaki, Waseda University, Japan
Krzysztof Szklanny, Polish-Japanese Academy of Information Technology, Poland
Christian M. Stracke, Open University of the Netherlands, The Netherlands
Ivan Ganchev, University of Limerick, Ireland / Plovdiv University "Paisii Hilendarski", Bulgaria
Tomayess Issa, Curtin University, Australia
Yifat Ben-David Kolikant, Hebrew University of Jerusalem, Israel
Mudasser Wyne, National University - San Diego, USA

eLmL Industry/Research Advisory Committee

Michael Verhaart, Eastern Institute of Technology Hawke's Bay, New Zealand
Guglielmo Trentin, Institute of Educational Technology of the Italian National Research Council (ITD-CNR), Italy

eLmL 2019 Technical Program Committee

Ali Ahmad Alawneh, Philadelphia University, Jordan
Yayoi Anzai, Kyushu University, Japan
Cristina Azevedo Gomes, Polytechnic Institute of Viseu, Portugal
Mohammed Bahja, University of Birmingham, UK
Juarez Bento da Silva, Universidade Federal de Santa Catarina, Brazil
Werner Beuschel, Technical University Brandenburg, Germany
Mohsin Bilal, Umm Al Qura University, Saudi Arabia
Gregory Bourguin, Université Littoral Côte d'Opale (ULCO), France
Julien Broisin, University of Toulouse, France
Eglė Butkevičienė, Kaunas University of Technology, Lithuania
José Carlos Metrolho, IPCB, Portugal
Maiga Chang, Athabasca University, Canada
Steven Chen, United Daily News, Taiwan
Lorraine Cleeton, Northcentral University / Walden University, USA
David Comiskey, Ulster University, Northern Ireland
André C. da Silva, Federal Institute of São Paulo - IFSP / NIED - UNICAMP, Brazil
Ana de las Heras, Udima Universidad a Distancia de Madrid, Spain
Giuliana Dettori, Istituto per le Tecnologie Didattiche, Genova, Italy
Ramon Fabregat Gesa, University of Girona, Spain
Daniel Farr, Kennesaw State University, USA
Joseph Finkelstein, Center for Bioinformatics and Health Analytics - Columbia University, USA
Sue Folley, University of Huddersfield, UK
Ivan Ganchev, University of Limerick, Ireland / Plovdiv University "Paisii Hilendarski", Bulgaria
Leonardo Garrido, Tecnológico de Monterrey, Mexico

Mahsa Ghasemi, University of Texas at Austin, USA
Henrique Gil, Escola Superior de Educação do Instituto Politécnico de Castelo Branco, Portugal
Lori Grata, Duquesne University / Yellow Wood Academy, USA
Wolfgang Greller, University College of Teacher Education Vienna, Austria
Giuliana Guazzaroni, Università Politecnica delle Marche, Italy
David Guralnick, Kaleidoscope Learning & Columbia University, New York, USA
Rawad Hammad, King's College London, UK
Felix Hamza-Lup, Georgia Southern University, USA
Feifei Han, University of Sydney, Australia
Abolfazl Hashemi, University of Texas at Austin, USA
Oriel Herrera, Universidad Católica de Temuco, Chile
Helen Hong, National Institute of Education, Singapore
Taketoshi Inaba, Tokyo University of Technology, Japan
Tsunenori Ishioka, The National Center for University Entrance Examinations, Japan
Tomayess Issa, Curtin University, Australia
Adel Jebali, Concordia University, Canada
Mike Joy, University of Warwick, UK
Alex Jung, Aalto University, Finland
Katerina Kabassi, TEI of Ionian Islands, Greece
Konstantinos Kalemis, Kapodistrian University of Athens, Greece
Keiichi Kaneko, Tokyo University of Agriculture and Technology, Japan
Charalampos Karagiannidis, University of Thessaly, Greece
Ilias Karasavvidis, University of Thessaly, Greece
Yifat Ben-David Kolikant, Hebrew University of Jerusalem, Israel
Bernd Krämer, FernUniversität in Hagen, Germany
Miroslav Kulich, Czech Technical University in Prague | Czech Institute of Informatics, Robotics, and Cybernetics, Czech Republic
Joseph C. Kush, Duquesne University, USA
Cynthia Y. Lester, Georgia State University, USA
Andreas Lingnau, Humboldt-Universität zu Berlin, Germany
Giorgos Liodakis, TEI of Crete, Greece
Martin Llamas Nistal, Universidade de Vigo, Spain
Josué Aarón López Leyva, CETYS Universidad, Mexico
Hwangji Sherrie Lu, Ashford University, USA
Luca Andrea Ludovico, Università degli Studi di Milano, Italy
Stefania Manca, Institute of Educational Technology - National Research Council of Italy, Italy
Flavio Manganello, ITD-CNR, Genoa, Italy
Giuseppina Rita Mangione, INDIRE (National Institute for Documentation, Innovation and Educational Research), Italy
Herwig Mannaert, University of Antwerp, Belgium
José Manuel Machado, University of Minho, Portugal
Davide Marocco, Universita' di Napoli Federico II, Italy
Alke Martens, University of Rostock, Germany
Paulo Martins, INESC TEC / University of Trás-os-Montes e Alto Douro, Portugal
Bruce R. Maxim, University of Michigan-Dearborn, USA
Natarajan Meghanathan, Jackson State University, USA
Santiago Mengual Andrés, University of Valencia, Spain
Alexander Mikroyannidis, Knowledge Media Institute | The Open University, UK

Begoña Montero-Fleta, Universitat Politecnica de Valencia, Spain
Rafael Morales Gamboa, Universidad de Guadalajara, Mexico
Umberto Nanni, Universita' di Roma "La Sapienza", Italy
Jari Palomaki, Tampere University of Technology - Pori, Finland
Andreas Papasalouros, University of the Aegean, Greece
Hugo Paredes, INESC TEC / University of Trás-os-Montes e Alto Douro, Portugal
Gerald Penn, University of Toronto, Canada
Arna Peretz, Ben-Gurion University of the Negev, Israel
Maria Potes Barbas, Escola Superior de Educação de Santarém, Portugal
Tamara Powell, Kennesaw State University, USA
Francesca Pozzi, Istituto Tecnologie Didattiche - CNR, Genoa, Italy
Athanasios Priftis, HES, Geneva, Switzerland
Natālija Prokofjeva, Riga Technical University, Latvia
Yannis Psaromiligkos, Piraeus University of Applied Science, Greece
Maja Pušnik, University of Maribor, Slovenia
Sonja D. Radenkovic, University of Belgrade, Serbia
Juliana Elisa Raffaghelli, University of Florence, Italy
Thurasamy Ramayah, Universiti Sains Malaysia, Malaysia
Fabrizio Ravicchio, ITD-CNR, Italy
Laura Rayón, Universidad de Alcalá, Spain
Miguel Angel Redondo Duque, Universidad de Castilla - La Mancha, Spain
Fernando Reinaldo Ribeiro, Polytechnic Institute of Castelo Branco, Portugal
Jan Renz, Hasso Plattner Institute | University of Potsdam, Germany
Marina Rui, University of Genova, Italy
Demetrios Sampson, Curtin University, Australia
Juan Manuel Santos Gago, University of Vigo, Spain
Maya Satratzemi, University of Macedonia, Thessaloniki, Greece
Carol Savill-Smith, Education Support Partnership, UK
Filippo Sciarrone, University of Roma Tre, Italy
Karim Sehaba, Université Lumière Lyon 2, France
Chihiro Shibata, Tokyo University of Technology, Japan
Jirarat Sitthiworachart, Walailak University, Thailand
Eliza Stefanova, Sofia University St. Kl. Ohridski, Bulgaria
Monika Steinberg, Hochschule Hannover, Germany
Christian M. Stracke, Open University of the Netherlands, The Netherlands
Boštjan Šumak, University of Maribor, Slovenia
Jakub Swacha, University of Szczecin, Poland
Krzysztof Szklanny, Polish-Japanese Academy of Information Technology, Poland
John T. Thompson, Buffalo State College, USA
Lisette Toetenel, Oxford Brookes University, UK
Jean-Philippe Trabichet, Haute Ecole de Gestion de Genève, Switzerland
Guglielmo Trentin, Institute of Educational Technology of the Italian National Research Council (ITD-CNR), Italy
Thrasyvoulos Tsiatsos, Aristotle University of Thessaloniki, Greece
Carlos Vaz de Carvalho, Instituto Superior de Engenharia do Porto, Portugal
Esteban Vázquez-Cano, Spanish National University of Distance Education (UNED), Spain
Ioanna Vekiri, independent writer and researcher, Greece
Michael Verhaart, Eastern Institute of Technology Hawke's Bay, New Zealand

Copyright Information

Augmented Reality Application for Telecommunications Concepts Learning

Patricia Madrinan
i2t Research group–CENIT Research Center
Universidad Icesi
Cali, Colombia
e-mail: patri@elsitiomio.com

Domiciano Rincon
i2t Research group
Universidad Icesi
Cali, Colombia
e-mail:
domiciano.rincon@correounivalle.edu.co

Andres Navarro
i2t Research group–CENIT Research Center
Universidad Icesi
Cali, Colombia
e-mail:anavarro@icesi.e.,du.co

***Abstract*—Learning concepts is difficult using only a traditional chalkboard approach; practical experience to develop enigineering abilities, however, can be expensive and complex. In this setting, a gamification approach is useful and can improve the learning process. The objective of this paper is to present an educational experience based on a technological development that is implemented on a smartphone using augmented reality. The purpose of this approach is to facilitate learning by maintaining the attention and interest of users/learners through game techniques, and to develop soft skills, such as teamwork and lifelong learning.**

Keywords-games; serious games; engineering education; gamification.

I. Introduction

Soft skills, such as teamwork, communication, and lifelong learning are essential for today's engineers but are fairly difficult to employ and evaluate. In addition, some concepts in radio engineering are traditionally taught in the classroom using a mathematical and theoretical approach. In this study, we propose a new approach for learning a traditional concept: radio localization, or direction finding (DF). Radio localization using line of bearing is a well known concept that has been described in the literature. However, our field experience has demonstrated that although many engineers understand the concept theoretically, they are unable to use DF equipment to locate an emitter. The use of portable DF equipment and illegal emitters is expensive, and there are regulations that prohibit the use of real test scenarios for training engineering students.

As a consequence of these limitations, we have developed an application called Hunting, with the aim of developing not only technical skills pertaining to DF concepts, but also soft skills, such as teamwork. Hunting refers to a task in telecommunications that involves using the line of bearing technique to locate a radio transmitter with a portable device. It should be noted that commercial devices for this purpose are sold by main test equipment manufacturers.

Telecommunications, within the context of engineering, encompasses a wide range of specific areas. It is a multidisciplinary field whose specific language must be decipherable by teams having different levels of abilities. Presenting an application in this field in a friendly and effective manner has been an incentive and challenge for our work.

Engineers, and more specifically engineering students, require skills that allow them to experiment proactively to acquire long-term learning abilities; simply acquiring knowledge that expires in a short time does not suffice. Each educational experience can be an opportunity to ask questions, make decisions, and dare to challenge previous assumptions.

The Hunting application serves to teach the basic concepts of DF. It is a serious multiplayer educational game that is developed as an application for Android cell phones using augmented reality. It integrates hardware capabilities to enable interaction with the application in the cloud, which can be remotely controlled by an instructor from a server, locating users in real time and adjusting the location of the goal.

The cognitive objective is very specific: to locate a source of interference. To accomplish this task, the apprentices must leave the classroom, or the enclosure, to find the source, aided by sounds, animations, and a dynamic map in the application. A clear goal, sense of achievement, deciphering an enigma, and conquering an objective are the essential components for maintaining motivation within the game, all while discovering and learning concepts in a pleasant and satisfying way.

With respect to technological devices, different levels of intimacy exist. The cell phone has become an extension of the body and is perceived as part of the individual, a prosthesis without which life seems unthinkable. This phenomenon occurs mainly among young people, who appear as true cybernetic organisms, or "cyborgs" [1]. A new category of educational mediation based on modern information and communication technologies has emerged, taking advantage of widespread smartphone use. Combining gameplay, usability, interactivity, and empathy, these afore-mentioned educational technologies can provide a friendlier learning environment than has so far been available.

Removing students from the classroom and including physical movement within a learning activity involves new challenges. The main objective of the proposed learning activity is to use a technological tool to help break the habits of passive learning and to force students to be active participants in the learning process.

Hardware limitations present several development challenges, however, such as the lack of standardization in the technical specifications of various commercial smartphone models. The link between mobile devices, which are increasingly affordable for the vast majority of the population, and new technologies gives rise to opportunities that transcend geographical distance and digital gaps. In this work, these opportunities are applied to education in the realm of engineering.

The remainder of this paper is organized as follows. In Section II, we describe the application and related concepts. In Section III, we present several technical matters and preliminary results obtained from a small group of students and individuals of different ages. In Section IV, we present conclusions and proposals for future work.

II. EXAMPLE OF "LIEs" MEDIATED BY A TECHNOLOGICAL APPLICATION

With our hunting application, we introduce the concept of a learning immersive experience significant (LIES), a proposal for an educational methodology that takes into account the experience of the individual and uses an application as a technological mediator. We play with the word *lies* (from the verb *lie*) to express that a virtual, or unreal world, using augmented reality (immersive experience) is used to enhance the learning experience (significant experience).

We propose a blended immersive approach, attempting to make use of traditional online virtual courses. However, our approach is neither a typical face-to-face course nor a virtual or traditional blended concept. Instead, it falls between both of these teaching methods, supposing a pedagogical mediator. On the one hand, there is mobile technology, which offers, similarly to tattoos or prostheses [2], an ever-present companion that accompanies individuals everywhere. On the other hand, there is the instructor, who provides a pedagogical experience by guiding a group in an adventure. The pedagogical figure has a great significance in all types of "disciplines" (which is received from another individual), in contrast to "invention" (which is discovered by oneself) [3].

Technology acts as the pedagogical mediator [4] between the cognitive content of the course and the interpersonal relationship between different participants of the same experience. It facilitates situations, triggers emotional responses, and generates circumstances that extend the boundaries of traditional education [5].

Fear is a barrier that can stop the immersion that enables the empowerment of knowledge [6]. However, the playfulness conspires to deal with the initial fear and overcome it. Through the game, we can appreciate the way in which the intangible becomes visible through a mediating device (augmented reality) when paying attention to signals and directions that guide us toward an objective. The relationship between the digital map and the terrain that we tread and the encounter with physical experiences related to a mental process generates an educational atmosphere that increases the level of consciousness and, therefore, the ability and autonomy to solve problems. A LIES search aims to make the apprentice, gamer, or user desire to learn and experience the following: "Instead of resisting or being scared when facing a task, we softly accomplish it, alive and fulfilled with new knowledge, and avid to see what comes next" [7].

The Hunting application is not a competitive game. All students must decipher the enigma (the location of the emitter), and collaboration is promoted when a team of two or more students share a device. The goal is clear: the students must locate the pirate (illegal emitter), which is the interference source responsible for generating problems (represented by a parrot as a figurative image of the target to be located). Hunting tasks involve DF issues, in which engineers must discover the precise location of the source on a map and travel to that location to retrieve it. With the Hunting application, students are immersed in the combination of the real world and the virtual world (as the information is generated in the application), and they must physically travel around the campus to find the emitter.

III. TECHNICAL FINDINGS AND PRELIMINARY RESULTS

The Hunting application requires an Internet connection, a cell phone with a global positioning system, and at least one of the following three sensors to be able to operate: digital compass; magnetic field sensor; and/or orientation sensor. The application uses an accelerometer to determine the position of the cell phone with respect to its center, and it uses the orientation sensor to determine the position of the cell phone with respect to the earth's north (and in this way, determine the direction in which the device points). Initially, we expected that most mid- to high-end devices would incorporate the required sensors, as they are used in many popular navigation applications.

The application was tested with various devices, including Huawei P8, Lenovo Vibe K5, Motorola Moto G2, Motorola Moto G3, Motorola Moto G4 plus, Motorola Moto X, Motorola Moto Z, Samsung Galaxy S6 Edge, and Samsung Galaxy Alpha. Of these cell phones, all the high-end phones were compatible with the application; that is, they possessed the required sensors. However, game performance in all cases was not identical. Samsung phones were expected to have superior performance, but their orientation sensor offered lower resolution by launching as few angles as possible when making a loop with the cell phone. Motorola Moto G2 and G4, Moto X, Huawei P8, and Lenovo Vibe K5 offered superior resolution in their orientation sensors, achieving improved performance by improving fluidity when making a sweeping motion looking for the "pirate." In contrast, to our surprise, Motorola Moto G3 and G4 Plus were not compatible with the application because they lacked an orientation sensor. We expected them to possess the sensor, as they were newer versions of the Moto G2 that did possess the orientation sensor. Finally, it should be noted that for correct operation of the orientation sensor, the mobile device must be shaken in all directions before starting the game.

Until now, we had only tested the application in a small group of undergraduate students to obtain an initial impression of the user experience. For the majority of the students, the use was intuitive, and all teams found the emitter. Some students had comments about the initial instructions; however, the application purposely lacks instructions. Because the game is intended not only for engineering students, but also for individuals from different telecommunications disciplines, the friendliness of the interface is important for facilitation of usability. Figure 1 demonstrates the initial screen of the application, and Figuress. 2 and 3 display students playing the game. In both figures, it is possible to see the various lines of bearing that are generated by the simulated direction finder in the application.

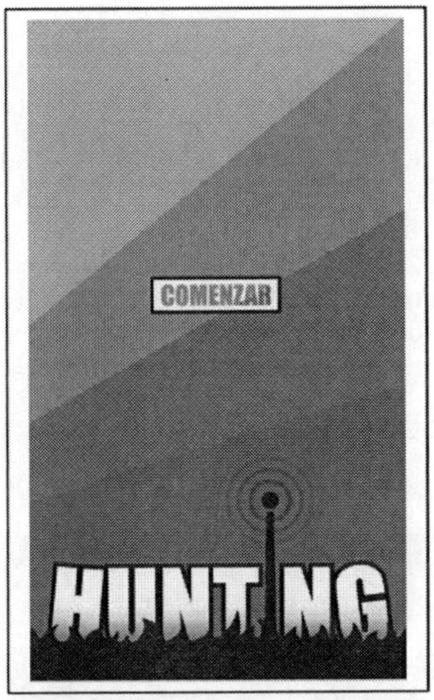

Figure 1. Welcome image of the application

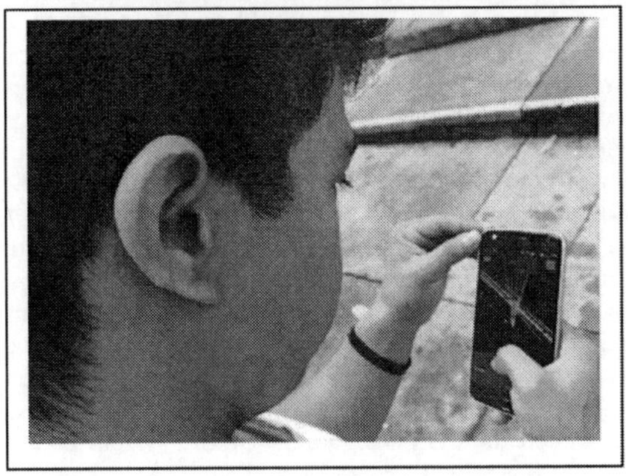

Figure 2. Student testing the application

Figure 3. Searching for the target.

IV. CONCLUSIONS

The educational experience process is the pedagogical objective itself, where the goal of the game is the excuse and learning is an additional gain. The important issue is the involvement of the skills necessary to achieve the goal and the manner in which this goal is achieved.

For the first time we propose and apply in this work the LIES concept using the Hunting application. This application of the LIES method, as a pedagogical mediation exercise using a technological development, is an example of a user-centered activity that offers a simple way of active learning, bypassing usual procedures by breaking away from the boundaries of the classroom.

Although technology serves as a mediator of the pedagogical process, it is not the center of the experience, but rather a tool. Requiring the application of knowledge, and transcending traditional classroom borders, the application allows for the integration of cognitive abilities and active learning. The LIES approach promotes the active role of the student, as students are eager to receive feedback that clarifies their experience. The Hunting application opens the door to learning, offering an autonomous exploratory activity.

One implementation problem of the Hunting application involves the differences in the performances of device sensors, as well as the lack of standardization in the technical specifications of different smartphone models. This issue results in different yields and accuracy of location data, and should be addressed in future work.

REFERENCES

[1] M. M. Kusnagi, "Dispositivos, prótesis y artefactos de la subjetividad cíborg," *Jóvenes Tecnofilosofía Arte Digit.*, p. 41, 2013.
[2] H. Belting, *Cruce de miradas con las imágenes. La pregunta por la imagen como pregunta por el cuerpo.* Universidad de Salamanca, 2011.
[3] E. D. Dussel, *La pedagógica latinoamericana.* Nueva América, 1980.
[4] F. G. Pérez and D. P. Castillo, *Mediación Pedagogica: apuntes para una educación a distância alternativa.* Instituto de Investigaciones y Mejoramiento Educativo, 1996.
[5] M. McLuhan, B. R. Powers, and C. Ferrari, *La aldea global.* Gedisa, 1995.
[6] J. A. Marina, *Anatomía del miedo.* Anagrama, 2010.
[7] C. Pinkola, *Mujeres que corren con los lobos.* Barcelona: Ediciones B, S.A., 1998

Reading Behaviors of Japanese Learners Based on Logs Recorded by Users of Digital Books

Teiko Nakano
Shobi University
Saitama, Japan
email: t-nakano@b.shobi-u.ac.jp

Teruko Harada
EF International Language Center
Tokyo, Japan
email: terukoharada@r7.dion.ne.jp

Abstract—**In this paper, the reading behaviors of Japanese learners in the upper intermediate level were analyzed according to reading time, amount of reading, dictionary use, the results of pre- and post-vocabulary tests, and the results of a quiz about the book that the learners read. Data on reading time, amount of reading, and dictionary use were collected from the learners' reading logs recorded on *BookLooper*, an application for viewing digital books. Results show that the learners who had read more understood the contents better and read faster than those who had read less. Furthermore, learners appeared to learn vocabulary incidentally in a virtuous circle of reading; once they enter that circle, they need to read books that are appropriate to their vocabulary level.**

Keywords-extensive reading; reading behaviors; virtuous circle; good reader; incidental vocabulary learning.

I. Introduction

Extensive reading is an approach of second language learning that improves language ability in a pleasurable way [1][2]. In particular, extensive reading using graded readers, where learners can repeatedly encounter unknown words, has an effect on learners in which they learn vocabulary incidentally [3]-[6]. Incidental vocabulary learning happens when words are learned by way of guessing because of repeated exposure to them in context while reading. In the process where unknown words become known words, there is a stage where learners recognize they have seen a word even though they do not know its meaning [7].

Day and Bamford [8] suggested that extensive reading can be included in a second language curriculum as an extracurricular activity. If the learners can learn the target language through extensive reading as an extracurricular activity without teachers' support; and if there is an on-line system that substitutes for the teacher, the learners who study Japanese as a second language by themselves can enjoy extensive reading on-line and evaluate and improve their language skills. The authors of this paper have developed Japanese graded readers with their colleagues [9] based on extensive reading and graded readers in English [6][10], and a support system for Japanese extensive reading [11] to benefit learners who cannot have the support of a teacher.

A. Good Readers

Extensive reading is a good approach for building vocabulary knowledge; however, as Coady [7] mentioned, learners are not able to continue reading and learn new vocabulary when they lack the basic vocabulary required to continue reading books. Nuttall [12] called this a vicious circle. That is, learners who find themselves in this circle read slowly, do not feel enjoyment, and do not read more. On the other hand, learners become good readers when they are in a virtuous circle, wherein they understand the content better, they enjoy reading, they read faster, and they read more [12]. Good readers can read quickly and better understand content, and then they read more [12].

B. Behavior during Extensive Reading

In contrast to intensive reading, which teachers use as a part of instruction in a general classroom, extensive reading can be done at anytime and anywhere with books that learners choose. However, many of the studies on the effectiveness of extensive reading investigate reading records, comments about books, and questionnaires conducted in a classroom [13]-[15].

In a study on behavior during extensive reading using eye camera, Kumada and Suzuki [16] observed the eye movement of participants while they did extensive reading and found they fixed their eyes on words more often and longer towards the end of the experiments. In addition, Kumada [17] reported on the way readers' attention changed from words to content by analyzing protocol data using the think-aloud method. In these investigations, learners read books that were given to them by teachers during class time.

Nakano [11] evaluated the support system for Japanese extensive reading and found the system was useful for independent learners to engage in extensive reading by choosing books by themselves. From the post questionnaire, the researcher reported the participants of the study evaluated a page called the "Personal Page" on the system positively, because on this page they could confirm by their reading logs what books they had read and how quickly they had read them [11]. The study also showed that those who read more and faster were from the group of participants whose Japanese proficiency level was higher [11]. However, the researcher did not find a relationship between reading speed and motivation. Are these participants who read more and faster good readers in Nuttall's [12] terms? What are the characteristics of their reading behavior? Reading behavior data could suggest ways of supporting learners to become good readers.

C. Study Questions

To find out how the learners of Japanese behave during extensive reading outside the classroom without a teacher's assistance, this study used a *BookLooper* to record learners' reading logs. *BookLooper* is an application for viewing digital teaching materials. Ogata et al. [18] revealed common learning behavior of the first-year university students whose grades went up by analyzing the amount of reading recorded on *BookLooper* and the time of day when they read. With this system, it is also possible to record other reading behavior such as the way that students open books, turn pages, turn back to previous pages, take notes, mark unknown words, and close books.

Therefore, this study examines the following questions:

1. Is there a difference in reading speed between learners who read more and learners who read less?
2. How do learners who read faster and understand content better behave, and how do learners who do not read faster and do not understand content better behave?

In Section II, the purpose and method of this study will be explained. Then, in Section III, the results will be discussed. In Section IV, the study will be concluded. In Section V, the study's limitations and further work will be discussed.

II. Purpose and Method

Here, we will introduce the purpose and the participants and then, explain the methodology of the study and the reading materials, vocabulary tests, questionnaires, and quizzes used. Lastly, we will show the reading logs.

A. Purpose

The purpose of this paper is to describe the behavior of good readers and to know the way good readers read in a virtuous circle by analyzing reading logs recorded by Japanese learners in the upper intermediate level.

B. Participants

Six international students (three male and three female) at three Japanese universities independently participated in this study. Their home countries included China (3), Vietnam (2), and Malaysia (1). As for the first language of the participants, four participants spoke languages that use Chinese characters, while two spoke languages that do not. Their Japanese learning experience ranged from 8 months to 30 months (average 23 months). To ascertain participants' Japanese abilities, they were asked to declare their recent Japanese proficiency levels, if they had taken a proficiency test on Japanese language. In order to assess their present level of Japanese vocabulary, the vocabulary section of a Japanese Language Proficiency Test (JLPT) was administered by the authors of this paper. The results are shown in Table I. The scores were calculated so that a perfect score would be 100.

TABLE I. Japanese Proficiency of Participants

ID	First Language	JLPT	Vocabulary
1	Chinese	N2	73
2	Chinese	-	61
3	Vietnamese	N2	80
4	Chinese	N2	86
5	Chinese	-	59
6	Vietnamese	N2	64

C. Method

Participants were required to read reading materials in the three holiday weeks from December 2016 to January 2017. They were then required to answer questions about the book and complete a questionnaire about the reading after they had finished reading each book. Pre- and post-vocabulary tests and questionnaires were conducted within a week before and after the reading. Data collection methods are shown in the following sections.

D. Reading Materials

As reading materials, a collection of Japanese graded readers [9], which is divided into eight levels from level A to H (beginner to upper intermediate levels), was used. They are written in Japanese using hiragana, katakana and kanji, but all the kanji words have hiragana written beside them to help learners read smoothly. Participants chose the specific titles on their own and read them on their own devices using *BookLooper* which provides reading materials in PDF. Since the titles the learners chose varied according to their interest, and one title read by all the participants was "Bocchan," this study investigates its reading logs. "Bocchan" is an E level reader (intermediate), and consists of 31,000 letters and 128 pages on PDF. PDF pages are fixed and do not reflow like E-Books. This means the contents of a page do not vary depending on the device used by a participant. While the length of English text is counted by words, the length of Japanese text is counted by the number of letters.

E. Pre- and Post-Vocabulary Test

To investigate whether participants had learned words used in books through reading, a vocabulary test on the collection of the present graded readers was prepared according to the below-mentioned procedure and conducted as pre- and post-vocabulary tests. In order to ensure that participants who do not use *kanji* in their first language were not at a disadvantage, all the test items were written without using *kanji*.

1. Depending on the word frequency in "Bocchan", low-frequency words, medium-frequency words, and high-frequency words were defined as being used 2-3, 4-9, and more than 10 times, respectively. Thirteen words (five low-frequency words, two medium-frequency words, and six high-frequency words) were chosen as test item words.
2. Ten dummy words that were not used in the book used in this study including "Bocchan" were chosen from the vocabulary list developed for writing graded readers [9].

Participants were asked to answer according to the following choices.

[a] This is the first time I have seen this word.

[b] I have seen this word before, but I do not know its meaning.

[c] I know the meaning of this word.

Referring to Coady [7], Grabe and Stroller [19], and Paribakht and Wesche [20], participants were asked to write the meaning in their first language when they chose [c]. To judge whether the meanings from [c] were correct, one of the authors and a translator whose first language was the same as that of the participant compared the answer to the previously prepared translation made by the translator.

F. Pre- and Post-Questionnaire

A questionnaire was administered before and after the research. In the pre-questionnaire, participants were asked about the following: self-assessment of their reading ability, difficulties in reading, interest in reading graded readers preferred language to read in (Japanese or one's first language), average reading amount in a month, and devices they usually use for reading digital books. Also, both in Japanese and their first language, they were asked whether they like to read and the genre of books they read. In the post-questionnaire, participants were asked which devices they had used to read in this study, their preference between paper and digital when reading, the effects of graded readers, and a comparison between graded readers and authentic books: (see Appendices A and B for complete versions).

G. Quizzes

To ascertain participants' understanding of the content, they were asked to answer five questions on each title using an online system [21]. Each question had four choices for answers and was used to gauge their reading comprehension. The system displays correct answers and the rate of correct answers after participants submit their answers.

H. Reading Logs

The following logs left by participants were collected by *BookLooper*.

1. Date and time of using specific functions: open (to open PDF file), close (to close PDF file), preview (to go back to a previous page), and next (to go on to the next page).
2. Words marked on *BookLooper* as "unknown words" and as "words looked up in a dictionary"
3. Comments inserted by participants when reading the book.

III. RESULTS

First, we will show the reading logs recorded by the participants and the number of new words they learned through reading. Then, we will discuss the relationship between Nuttall's circle and the behaviors of the participants. Lastly, we will discuss how the unknown words were learned.

A. Reading Logs

Table II shows the results of the reading logs. "ID" refers to each participant. "Page" means the number of the last continuous page the participants read. "Open" shows the number of times that participants opened books on their devices. "Preview" refers to the number of times that participants went back to the previous page. When the number of "Open" and "Preview" is higher, it means that the participant more frequently interrupted reading. "Unknown words" refers to the number of words that participants marked as unknown. "Dictionary" shows the number of words that participants marked as words that they looked up in a dictionary. As Day and Bamford [8] encouraged students not to use the dictionary while reading, the authors of this paper also encouraged participants not to use a dictionary unless they found it difficult to understand the passage without knowing the meaning of a certain word. "Time" refers to the total number of minutes spent on reading. "Time/Page" refers to how many minutes it took a student to read one page on average. "Variance" refers to how far a set of numbers are spread out from their average value. A high number tells us that a reader read at widely different speeds. For example, if we look at three participants, ID3, ID4, and ID6, we can see that their average reading speed was 1.8 minutes per page each. However, ID3 and ID6 varied widely in the span of time it took them to read different pages. "Variance" can show us what "Time/Page" cannot show us. Perhaps, ID6 became distracted while reading and this may explain why he/she gave up reading after 27 pages. It can be noted that participants who met many "Unknown" words and often used a "Dictionary" took more time than those who did not. Participants tended to need more time to read a page in the early part of a book compared to later pages. Participants most likely were not accustomed to *BookLooper* and did not have the background knowledge needed for the book in the first half. "Note" shows the frequency that participants inserted comments such as "it is interesting," "I was impressed," and "I do not understand" while reading.

TABLE II. READING LOG

ID	Page	Open	Preview	Unknown	Dictionary	Time	Time/ Page	Variance	Note
1	128	91	142	35	11	285	2.2	4.8	15
2	128	46	21	9	0	263	2.1	3.3	0
3	128	73	55	6	0	229	1.8	1.6	0
4	128	6	47	1	0	233	1.8	2.4	2
5	23	18	12	1	0	92	4.0	16.3	0
6	27	20	29	0	1	49	1.8	4.5	2

TABLE III. RESULTS OF PRE- AND POST-VOCABULARY TEST

ID	Quiz	Words actually used (13)				Dummy words (10)			
		1-1	1-0	0-1	0-0	1-1	1-0	0-1	0-0
1	80	1	0	2	10	0	0	0	10
2	60	0	0	5	8	0	0	0	10
3	80	4	1	1	7	0	1	0	9
4	80	5	0	2	6	0	0	0	10
5	-	1	1	0	11	0	0	0	10
6	40	3	0	2	8	2	0	0	8
Total		14	2	12	50	2	2	0	57

B. *Number of Words Learned*

Table III shows the results of pre- and post-vocabulary tests. "1" means that the answer for [c] was correct, and "0" means that the answer for [c] was incorrect. "0" also appears when answers were [a] or [b]. For example, "1-1" shows that participants answered correctly on both the pre- and post-vocabulary tests. In comparison between the words that were actually used and the dummy words, the answer set of "1-1" was found more in words that were actually used. It was to be expected that words that the participants already knew were used in the books, because the books were chosen based on their appropriateness to the vocabulary level of the participants. "1-0" shows that participants answered correctly before reading, and answered incorrectly after reading. There were two such results in this category, both in words that were actually used and in dummy words. "0-1" shows that participants answered incorrectly before reading, and correctly after reading. There were twelve such results in words that were actually used, as opposed to 0 in dummy words. This indicates that the participants learned the meaning of those words through reading.

C. *Virtuous and Vicious Circle of Reading*

When dividing participants into good readers (in the virtuous circle) and weak readers (in the vicious circle) based on Nuttall's [12] theory, ID1, ID3, and ID4 were considered to be good readers and ID5 and ID6 were considered to be weak readers. In addition, we found ID2 to be a reader "on the way to being a good reader."

The average reading time spent per page for the four participants (ID1, ID2, ID3, and ID4) who finished reading "Bocchan" was around 2 minutes (Table II). From the results shown in Table III, they understood 80% of the content, with the exception of ID2.

ID4 received the highest vocabulary score, 86, in Table I, and gave the highest number of known words (with an answer set of "1-1"), five, words that were actually used, as shown in Table III. Because the number for "Open" is lower, it can be inferred that ID4 concentrated while reading. ID4 also left the comments, "It was interesting," and, "It was sad." That is, ID4 had already become a good reader in the virtuous circle because ID4 knew many words, understood well, enjoyed reading, and read at a fast pace.

ID1 and ID3, who finished reading with an appropriate reading rate, were also good readers. It can be inferred that ID1 took more reading time than average because she went back to the previous page and marked many items with "Unknown" and "Dictionary." It is likely that the variance of ID1 was greater because the time spent on the page where marks were left tended to be longer. ID1 enjoyed the reading, leaving many comments such as "It was interesting," "I could laugh," and "I was impressed."

In contrast to these participants, ID2 lacked necessary vocabulary, receiving 61, the lowest vocabulary score in Table I. ID2's comprehension was slightly lower than other participants' because he received a grade of 60 in questions about the book. He opened 46 times, went back to a previous page 21 times, and didn't use dictionary. However, ID2 received a mark of 5 in "0-1" in words actually used in Table III, which was the highest. These results suggest that ID2 read by guessing the meaning of unknown words from context without going back to the previous page. Nuttall [12] said that any factor out of speed, enjoyment, and comprehension could provide the key to move students out of the vicious circle and into the virtuous one. ID2 read with appropriate speed and learned unknown words by guessing from their context. ID2's behavior shows the process of "on the way to being a good reader."

On the other hand, ID5 and ID6, who did not finish the reading, were considered as being in the vicious circle. These two participants answered "my reading ability is not good" in the pre-questionnaire. ID5 spent 4 minutes per page, which was the longest. ID5 received a vocabulary score of 59; it is likely that she encountered many unknown words while reading. However, she marked only one word as "Unknown," because she had read only 23 pages. ID5 answered "I prefer paper" to the question "How did you feel about the digital book compared to a paper book?"

ID6 took 1.8 minutes to read a page, which was short. The vocabulary score of ID6 was 64, and she read 27 pages. ID6 never marked "Unknown" and left the comment "I do not understand well" on page 4. Although ID6 had slightly more vocabulary than ID2, either she was not accustomed to reading on digital books or did not enjoy reading the book. ID6 answered the questions about the book although she had not finished it.

D. *How the Unknown Words were Learned*

To better understand the behavior of a participant who learned words during reading, the words marked on the *BookLooper* among the items of the vocabulary test are shown in Table IV, which shows ID1's results. The frequency of each word in the book is shown in parenthesis. ID1 marked "Dictionary" on "*shukuchoku* (night duty)" and "*batta* (a grasshopper)" and "Unknown" on "*kinodoku* (sorry)." In the pre-vocabulary test, ID1 answered [b: I have seen this word before, but I do not know its meaning] to "*shukuchoku*," however, he looked it up in a dictionary and answered correctly in the post-vocabulary test. For "*batta*" and "*kinodoku*," ID1 answered [a: This is the first time I have seen this word]. However, ID1 did not look them up in a dictionary, and answered [b] in the post-vocabulary test. It can be inferred that he guessed the meaning of the word because the illustration of "*batta*" was in the book. To "*kinodoku*," ID1 provided the words in his first language, "I am sorry, excuse me" in Japanese. Although the answer was judged to be incorrect through the discussion between one of the authors and the translator, it seems that she guessed a

TABLE IV. RESULTS OF PRE- AND POST-VOCABULARY TEST: WORDS WITH MARKS IN THE READING LOG

ID	*shukuchoku* (22)		*batta* (12)		*kinodoku* (8)	
	pre	post	pre	post	pre	post
1	b	1	a	b	a	0

similar meaning from the context. Although participants who got many "0-0" scores in Table III are considered to not have learned the words through reading, there may be cases similar to ID1, who had guessed a similar (but not exact) meaning from context.

IV. Conclusion

In this study, participants who finished reading are defined as "learners who read more pages" and participants who did not finish reading are defined as "learners who read fewer pages." In this section, first, we will discuss study question 1 and study question 2. Then, based on the behavior of ID2, we will discuss who was on the way to being a good reader, ways to support learners as they move into the virtuous circle.

A. Amount Read and Reading Rate

In comparison between the learners who read more and the learners who read less, the former took 2.0 minutes to read a page while the latter took 2.9 minutes. It can thus be said that learners who read more take less time to read than do learners who read less. That is, learners who read more read faster.

B. Reading Behaviors Shown in the Amount and Rate of Reading

Using the results of questions about books as ways to measure comprehension, it can be said that learners who read more, who gave 75% correct answers on average, understood the content. This, combined with the results of question 1, shows that "learners who can read faster and understand contents" read more. In that case, how did the readers who read slowly, and gave up reading after 20% of the book, understand the contents? The comprehension level of ID5 is unknown, because she did not answer the questions about the book. On the other hand, ID6 answered the questions about the book, and showed a 40% comprehension rate, and, in addition, learned words from the book. However, it may be that a lack of understanding caused her to stop reading because she left the comment "I do not understand well." Therefore, it can be said that "learners who cannot read faster and do not understand the content" read less.

C. Shift to a Good Reader

Among "learners who could read faster and understand the content," ID2 had a lower vocabulary level than the other learners, who had already become good readers (ID1, ID3, and ID4). Therefore, ID2's comprehension was slightly lower than that of the others. However, the number of words that he had learned through reading was the highest among participants. This shows that the level of reading material was appropriate for ID2. ID2 read with appropriate speed and learned the meaning of words incidentally by guessing meaning from the context. It has been said that more than 95% of words in the text should be known by readers in order for them to learn the meaning of unknown words by guessing from context [6][22][23]. The lack of vocabulary is considered to be the reason that ID5 and ID6 could not finish the reading. These results show that there are two categories among the learners who finished reading: learners who have already become good readers and those who are on their way to becoming good readers.

These results suggest that incidental vocabulary learning occurs for learners in the process of getting into the virtuous circle. At the same time, to enter the virtuous circle, learners need to read a book that is appropriate for their vocabulary level. In order to support learners as they move toward the virtuous circle to becoming good readers, providing a tool that can judge learners' vocabulary level is necessary in order to know the appropriate level of graded readers for them to start reading.

V. Limitations and Further Work

In this study, to describe the reading behavior of Japanese learners outside the classroom, logs on digital books recorded by participants were analyzed. From the results, the behavior of learners both in the virtuous circle and in the vicious circle, as defined by Nuttall [12], could be seen. In addition, the reading behavior of the learners with a lower vocabulary level, who continued reading by guessing the meanings of unknown words from context, shows that the process of moving into the virtuous circle can include incidental vocabulary learning. However, the results of this study cannot be generalized because of the small number of participants. Furthermore, participants' Japanese ability was assessed on the basis of vocabulary alone, but not in general. To improve the support system for Japanese extensive reading, a larger-scale study with more participants is needed to reveal the details of the virtuous circle of reading and the effect of vocabulary learning through extensive reading. This can be done by collecting more data from participants and giving a general assessment of their Japanese ability.

Acknowledgment

This work was supported by JSPS KAKENHI Grant Number 18K00694.

References

[1] I. S. P. Nation, Teaching ESL/EFL reading and writing. New York, NY: Routledge, 2009.

[2] S. D. Krashen, "Does free voluntary reading lead to academic language?,"Journal of intensive English studies, 11, pp. 1-18, 1997.

[3] K. Mikami and T. Harada, "Exploring the possibility of incidental vocabulary acquisition through extensive reading: From results based on extensive reading and vocabulary tests of Japanese graded readers," Japan Foundation Nihongo Kyoiku Kiyo, 7, pp. 7-21, 2011.

[4] R. Waring, "Why extensive reading should be an indispensable part of all language program?" The Language Teacher, 30 (7), pp. 44-47, 2006.

[5] M. Pigada and N. Schmitt, "Vocabulary acquisition from extensive reading: A case study'" Reading in a Foreign Language, 18 (1), pp. 1-28, 2006.

[6] I. S. P. Nation, Learning vocabulary in another language. Cambridge University Press, 2001.

[7] J. Coady, L2 vocabulary acquisition through extensive reading. In J. Coady and T. Huckin (Eds.), Second language vocabulary acquisition (pp. 225-237). Cambridge University Press, 1997.

[8] R. R. Day and J. Bamford, Extensive reading in the second language classroom. Cambridge University Press, 1998.

[9] B. Reynolds, T. Harada, M. Yamagata, and T. Miyazaki, "Towards a framework for Japanese graded readers: Initial research findings," Papers of the Japanese Langaugae Teaching Association in honor of Professor Fumiko Koide, 11, pp. 23-40, 2003.

[10] I. S. P. Nation, Teaching and learning vocabulary. Rowley, MA: Newbury House, 1990.

[11] T. Nakano, "Development of a support system for Japanese extensive reading: An evaluation of the system by learners," International Journal on Advances in Intelligent Systems, 10 (3&4), pp. 423-433, 2017.

[12] C. Nuttall, Teaching reading skills in a foreign language. Oxford, UK: Macmillan, 2005.

[13] M. Awano, K. Kawamoto, and M. Matsuda, Nihongo kyoshi no tameno tadoku nyumon. Tokyo, JAPAN: Ask, 2012.

[14] S. Matsui, K. Mikami, and Y. Kanayama, "A report on extensive reading in the basic and intermediate Japanese classes," The Research Center for Japanese Language Education International Christian University annual bulletin, 9, pp. 47-60, 2012.

[15] R. Ninomiya and M. Kawakami, "Effects of extensive reading on JSL learners' motivation," Journal of Global Education Hitotsubashi University, 3, pp. 53-65, 2012.

[16] M. Kumada and M. Suzuki, "The effectiveness of extensive reading on learners at the intermediate level of Japanese," Bulletin of Japanese Language Center for Internatinal Students Tokyo University of Foreign Studies, 39, pp. 31-48, 2013.

[17] M. Kumada, "Practice of extensive reading: Change in reading identified by talks," Bulletin of Japanese Language Center for Internatinal Students Tokyo University of Foreign Studies, 42, pp. 111-122, 2016.

[18] H. Ogata, C. Yin, M. Oi, F. Okubo, A. Shimada, K. Kojima and M. Yamada, "Analyses of learning behavior of active learners using logs of digital teaching materials," Bulletin of KIKAN Education Kyushu University, 2, pp. 48-60, 2016.

[19] W. Grabe and F. L. Stoller, "Reading and vocabulary development in a sedond languag: A case stydy. In J. Coady and T. Huckin (Eds.), Second language vocabulary acquisition (pp. 98-122). Cambridge University Press, 1997.

[20] T. S. Paribakht and M. Wesche, "Vocabulary enhancement activities and reading for meaning in second language vocabulary acquisition," In J. Coady and T. Huckin (Eds.), Second language vocabulary acquisition (pp.174-200). Cambridge University Press, 1997.

[21] T. Nakano, "Introduction of blended type extensive reading lessons using electronic reading materials," Shobi Journal of Policy Studies, 17, pp. 137-144, 2013.

[22] B. Laufer, "What percentage of text-lexis is essential for comprehension?," In C. Lauren and M. Nordman (Eds.), Special language: From humans thinking to thinking machines (pp.316-323). Cleavedon, UK: Multilingual Matters, 1989.

[23] B. Laufer, "The lexical plight in second language reading: Words you don't know, words you think you know, and words you can't guess," In J. Coady and T. Huckin (Eds.), Second language vocabulary acquisition (pp.20-34). Cambridge University Press, 1997.

APPENDIX A

Pre-Questionnaire

1. How would you describe your reading comprehension level? Why do you think that?
   a) Very good
   b) Good
   c) Fair
   d) Not good
   e) Bad
2. What is difficult for you when you read in Japanese? (you can choose more than two)
   a) Unknown words
   b) Pronunciation of *kanji*
   c) Grammar
   d) Other (please write in detail.)
3. Would you like to read graded readers?
   a) Would very much like to read
   b) Would like to read
   c) Yes and no
   d) Have no interest
4. Do you like to read? Please answer regarding both Japanese and your first language.
   a) Yes
   b) No
   c) I do not mind
5. What genre do you read? Please answer regarding both Japanese and your first language (you can choose more than two)
   a) Newspaper
   b) Novels
   c) Magazine
   d) Manga
   e) Other (please write in detail)
6. Which language do you read in the most?
   a) Japanese
   b) Your first language
   c) Almost the same
7. How many books do you read in a month on average? Please answer regarding both Japanese and your first language.
   a) 0
   b) 1-2
   c) 3-4
   d) 5-6
   e) 7-9
   f) more than 10
8. Which devices do you use when you read a digital book?
   a) Tablet
   b) Smartphone
   c) PC
   d) Other

Appendix B

Post-Questionnaire

1. Which devices did you use to read digital books? (you can choose more than two)
   a) Tablet
   b) Smartphone
   c) PC
   d) Other
2. Do you prefer paper books or digital books and why? Please choose one from A, B, or C. Please write why you chose A, B, or C.
   a) Paper books
   b) Digital books
   c) I do not care
3. Do you think that graded readers will be effective in improving your reading comprehension, if you continue extensive reading?
   a) It really helps to improve my reading ability.
   b) It helps to improve my reading ability a little bit.
   c) My reading ability will not change.
   d) Other (Please write a comment)
4. If you answered a) or b) in 3, what do you think the effect of ER is? (you can choose more than two)
   a) Extensive reading helps me to learn words.
   b) Extensive reading helps me to learn how to read *kanji*.
   c) Extensive reading helps me to understand contents without a dictionary.
   d) Other (please write a comment.)
5. Could you read graded readers with the same ease as stories written in your first language?
   a) I could read graded readers with the same ease as stories written in my first language.
   b) I could read graded readers more easily than stories written in my first language.
   c) I read graded readers with more difficulty than stories written in my first language.
   d) Other (please write a comment)
6. Do you prefer graded readers or general books written for native Japanese people? Please explain.
   a) Graded readers
   b) Books written for native Japanese people
   c) I do not care
   d) Other (please write a comment)

An Active Learning Approach for Teaching Web Development- Action Research Study

Mohammed Bahja
School of Computer Science
University of Birmingham
Birmingham, United Kingdom
E-mail: m.bahja@bham.ac.uk

Mitul Shukla
School of Computer Science and Technologies
University of Bedfordshire
Luton, United Kingdom
E-mail: mitul.shukla@beds.ac.uk

Abstract— **This paper presents an Action Research study for incorporating new learning and teaching methods into a Web Development module at a U.K. University, addressing the problems of varied experiences amongst the students with programming languages and computational thinking. Active learning concepts were introduced using three experiments involving Learning by Teaching, Jigsaw Puzzle, and Observations from Videos. These experiments were aimed at enhancing the students learning capabilities and computational thinking. All three experiments have achieved positive results among the students who were evaluated using formative assessments during their practical sessions. The study has found that Active Learning concepts can enhance student learning capabilities and give them more control over their own learning.**

Keywords- Action Research; Active Learning; Teaching; Web development

I. INTRODUCTION

Action Research in education, unlike other approaches focuses on ways of identifying strategies to improve skills and techniques of the researcher/teacher so that effective delivery methods can be incorporated into the teaching according to the various issues identified with the students. For example, qualitative and quantitative approaches or a mixed approach including both qualitative and quantitative may be effective in analyzing a particular issue or context, but they lack a collaborative and a democratic approach, which can be identified in Action Research [1] [2] [3]. In addition, Action Research offers a continued reflection on a problem or issue, where the goal is continuous improvement of the processes to address the problems [3]. Further, Action Research focuses on doing things better rather than investigating why we do those said things, and on identifying and adopting a change in teaching methods to achieve a positive impact for students [8]. A more detailed explanation of Action Research was identified in the works of Watts [23], which states that Action Research is a disciplined inquiry done by a teacher within the context of a teaching environment that would identify and inform the changes to be adopted in the teaching practice/methods. It is a continuous practice that has to be adopted by teachers to identify the solutions to changing problems and to deliver the best and most effective educational outcome.

According to Watts [23], the objectives/practices of Action Research in teaching and learning processes include the following:

- Educators should work best themselves on identifying problems in the teaching environment.
- Educators should be more effective in identifying problems and considering ways of working differently, which could be more effective compared to more traditional methods.
- These processes should also aim for professional development.
- A collaborative approach has to be practiced involving students and other teachers in identifying best practices.

It is also essential to understand the characteristics of Action Research that makes it unique and different from other research practices. Various characteristics of Action Research were identified in [22], highlighting it as an innovative and continuous approach, which is strategically driven, participatory in nature, adopting an intervention approach by implementing a solution to the problem identified, and the whole process is documented, understood and disseminated. Therefore, Action Research is different from scientific research in many aspects including the objective, methodology and the motivation and purpose. Action researchers typically do not use complex statistical procedures involved in quantitative research to evaluate results; however, they do offer other evidence (such as comparison with similar data) in order to prove that their measures are reliable and valid [3]. Action Research is focused on continuous reflection and improvement rather than focusing on the final outcome or conclusion, as observed in many scientific research studies. Various studies [29]-[32] have implemented the action research methods, and found it very useful in the long-term process. In the study performed in [29], inquiry-based classroom discussions were used as a method for developing the higher order cognitive skills among the chemistry students. Similarly, action research methodology can also be used for analyzing and promoting the learning process of students in computing programming module in a blended learning environment [30]. Similarly, online journals learning was used as an approach in the study performed in [31] through action research for promoting the learning computer applications and network programming. Other approaches such as Boolean Ninja, Minimum Spanning tree were used as the part of study in [32] for developing the critical thinking and computational abilities among the computing students. The approaches adopted in these studies were depending on their objective and the areas of problems identified. However, the aspects of collaborative approaches and active involvement in action research were not focused to a great extent in the research studies relating to the computing programming modules.

The Action Research process involves various stages. Different authors have described different stages, which can be summarized into the five main stages [8] as shown in the

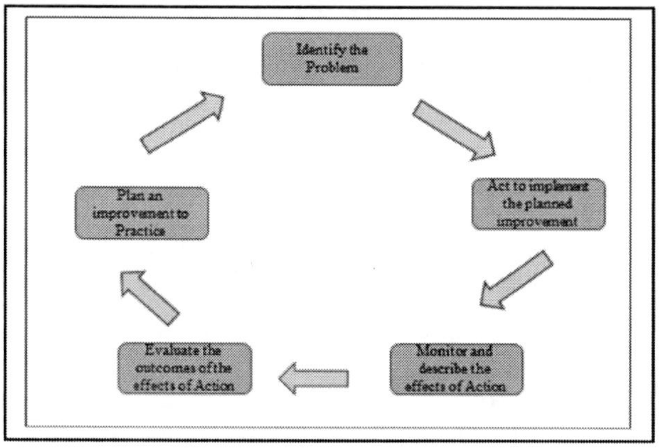

Figure 1. Stages of Action Research

The five stages explained are used for identifying the problems and conducting the Action Research using various techniques. The impact of these techniques including 'learning by teaching', 'jigsaw technique', and 'video observations and reactions' on the learning and development process of the web development students is investigated in this study.

The rest of the paper is structured as follows. In Section 2, we present the design and the process of action research with web development students, which included the problem identification, improvement planning process, implementing and monitoring the actions, evaluating the effects of the planned actions, and planning the improvement. In Section 3, we present the limitations and challenges observed in this study; and Section 4, concludes the study.

II. Action Research with Web Development Students

The web development module is a comprehensive course which is designed to educate the students with the various technologies used in the web design and development. The course syllabus can be summarized under the following points.

- Responsive web design using HTML5 and CSS3
- Web Information Architecture and Content Management Systems
- Web development using Java along with underlying technologies including C#, C++, ASP, LINQ
- Client-side and Server-side Programming
- Patterns and methods to enhance maintainability and testability
- Applying business logic
- Testing, deployment and configuration
- Performance modelling and management

The aim of this course is to educate the students in all the major spheres of web development and management. Accordingly, the teaching process focuses on programming and coding to the large extent with the regular lectures explaining the major concepts.

In order to incorporate Action Research techniques into the teaching process and improving the skills and educational outcomes of Web Development students, a strategic approach was formulated which is explained in the following sections.

A. Problem Identification

One of the important stages of Action Research is the identification of the problem. There are various approaches such as questionnaire surveys, interviews, observations, checklists etc. that are available for identifying the problem by involving the population in reflecting their opinions [27]. However, surveys and interviews are the most commonly used approaches in this process; surveys can be used to assess and identify the issues, while interviews can be used for in-depth analysis of the issues or problems [28]. It is necessary to identify students learning issues related to the module, and also the topics which cannot be understood by the students, so that the effective learning strategies can be planned and implemented.

In order to assess and understand the problems faced by students in understanding the concepts of a Web Development module, a questionnaire-based survey was carried out. The questionnaire was designed with ten questions in two sections. The first section had six questions focusing on the student abilities, where they are required to answer the topics which their awareness, expertise and experience related to various topics in the web development module. The second section had four questions related to the learning abilities and their feedback of using different approaches in teaching, such as collaborative approach. All the students attending the module (30: 19 males; 11 females) participated in the survey. Among the 30 students, 22 students belonged to the age group 20-25 years; and eight students in 25-30 years age group. After analysing the survey responses, it was identified that the lack of experience in programming languages and computational thinking skills among students were the main problems affecting their understanding of the concepts in Web Development. These problems are mostly focused on the students past learning and abilities. Such problems require active involvement of students in learning on their own and making them responsible, confident and able to take charge of their own learning. Considering the case, Active Learning methods and techniques were identified as the best strategy for achieving the effective educational outcomes.

Active learning is a process of engaging students in the learning process using different techniques. Unlike a more traditional approach where students might listen while lecturers explain, Active Learning requires the engagement of students in various learning activities through collaboration. In [6], it was stated that students must do more than just listen, which includes reading, writing, discussing and engaging in solving problems, and adopt higher order thinking in tasks, such as analysis, synthesis and evaluation. In short, students are involved in doing learning activities, thinking about the concepts and also what they are doing. Several studies have shown greater improvement among the students by adopting Active Learning techniques [17]-[19].

In Active Learning, students are constantly processing what they are learning through discussions, debating, writing short notes etc. Various benefits have been identified by the authors in different settings. Interactive courses were found to be more effective in promoting conceptual understanding as compared to traditional courses [11]. In addition, the meta-analysis of 225 studies across STEM (Science, Technology, Engineering & Mathematics) conducted in [10] has found that average exam scores of the students were improved by 6% by adopting Active Learning classes; and also, students following traditional lectures were 1.5 times more likely to fail compared to the students following Active Learning classes.

Computational Thinking is one of the effective techniques used in problem solving, application development, system designing etc. It can be effectively applied in both computer programing courses and also in other courses [20]. It includes the use of various techniques such as decomposition (breaking down data into smaller parts), pattern recognition (observing patterns/regularities), abstraction, designing etc. [24]. Realizing its importance, The International Society for Technology in Education (ISTE), Computer Science Teachers Association (CSTA) and the UK Computing at School working group (CAS) have collaborated with representatives from education and industry to develop computational thinking resources for educators [21].

Considering these factors, using Active Learning methods in teaching practices for a Web Development module could help to solve the problem and increase students' achievements. Thus, the following research question was formulated.

How can we use Active Learning methods and techniques to mitigate the problem of different skill sets and capabilities by helping the student to be in charge of their own learning?

B. Planning an implementation of Improvement

An action plan usually involves the process of deciding a new strategy or approach for addressing research questions; identifying the data needed to learn about the research questions; framing an approach or timeline for implementing the new strategy; and a plan for evaluating the findings from deploying the new strategy [5] [16].

Accordingly, the problems and the interests of the students from the Web Development module were identified using a questionnaire-based survey as explained in the previous section. The subsequent data analysis has shown that the students were interested in adopting Active Learning techniques for addressing their concerns and enhancing their skills and learning capabilities. Considering these outcomes, the approaches in teaching should be focused on actively involving the students in the learning process. Learning by teaching is one such approach, which directly involves the students in learning the concepts by teaching. In addition, as the students attending the module are from different regions with varying learning abilities, collaborative approaches can be very effective in the process of learning [2]. However, there is a need for approach that requires collective efforts of all the students in the learning process, so that all the students can be benefitted from these approaches. In addition, as discussed in the introduction, the use of collaborative approaches was not explored to a great extent in the computing learning environments. Therefore, approaches such as, learning by teaching, Jigsaw Puzzle, and Video observations were selected as a part of this study. Accordingly, three rounds of experiments were planned over a period of three weeks with each session of 3 hours duration. Each experiment used Active Learning techniques to deliver the concepts relating to each chapter of the Web Development module. A formative assessment was used for evaluating the experiment which focused on using the programming exercises during practical sessions.

a. **Experiment 1: Learning by Teaching**

Learning by teaching is an effective Active Learning technique that has been widely recognized and tested [9]. It is a process where students are asked to teach the concepts of a particular subject or chapter in a class which would be monitored by a teacher and corrected if necessary. This process actively involves the students in the learning process as they feel more responsible in explaining the concepts and more attentive due to the social presence in the class room. This approach was found to be more effective compared to other techniques like re-study or writing [12]. Therefore, using this technique, the students from the Web Development module were asked to teach the concepts of HTTP Methods in the class room. The effectiveness of the experiment was evaluated during the practical sessions.

b. **Experiment 2: The Jigsaw Technique**

The Jigsaw Technique is a form of teaching strategy adopting principles of cooperative learning that helps students to develop skills for effectively working in teams or in collaboration with one another. It focuses on cooperation rather than competition among students and is one of the most supported techniques within the education field as evidenced by more than 1200 research studies [15]. It helps students to understand a concept, apply the language of the discipline and practice self and peer teaching [7]. The technique usually gives a common task to all the students/teams. These students/ teams initially have to solve a problem and identify the relevant issues, which they later discuss with other students/teams. After collaborating with other students and identifying different issues, the best possible solution is formulated by those students for addressing the common task.

Using this technique, the students from a Web Development module were given a task (piece of puzzle), which initially they need to solve on their own. Later they need to collaborate with other students to find the most effective solution to the puzzle. The puzzle is about building the most effective algorithm to travel from the University main compass to a local international airport. This task gave students the idea of designing an algorithmic solution to a given real life problem through individual thinking and team work. This approach would also enhance the students computational thinking capabilities, as well as training them in the process of simplifying complex problems into simpler issues by breaking the problem down into smaller parts. This approach was then evaluated during practical sessions.

c. **Experiment 3: Videos Observation and Reaction**

Using multimedia content in teaching has been widely practiced across various institutions [13]. It has many benefits compared to traditional modes of teaching [25]. Using videos for teaching and enabling students to observe the important aspects from those videos is one of the techniques used to increase student observation skills and understanding various issues [4]. Studies have proved that videos can be used effectively in teaching and can attract students' attention and improve their skills [26].

Using video as a tool for observational learning, students from a Web Development module were given carefully chosen short videos from the Big Bang Theory comedy series to watch. These videos were related to team work, collaborative working, and project management. The students were distributed into two groups. The first group was assigned with the task of identifying the positive things from the videos; and the second group for identifying the negative things, which they would link to their group projects and assignments. This experiment was then evaluated during practical sessions.

C. Monitoring and describing the effects of the actions

All of the three experiments were carefully monitored and the observations were recorded. In the first experiment (Learning by Teaching), the students were asked to teach HTTP Methods, both GET and POST functions to be used in the Web development and also how the HTTP request cycle operates (the module concepts which the students found difficult in programming: observed from survey results). Though the students were initially nervous, they were able to quickly adapt to the teaching technique and reflected their understanding of these concepts in an effective way. Some corrections and suggestions were made to the students while they were teaching to boost their confidence and correct their mistakes.

The second experiment (Jigsaw Technique) was used for enhancing the computational thinking of students. Majority of the students (76%) stated that they face problems in designing the sorting algorithms. To address this issue, the students were asked to build the most effective algorithm to travel from the University main campus to a local international airport; first by working individually, and then in collaboration. The experiment was monitored and tips were given to students while working in groups on identifying the main points and issues in formulating the best possible route.

Another important issue identified from the survey results was that, 86% of the students had problems in identifying the right requirements and reflecting them in the coding. As this process requires the identification of right set of tools and commands in coding, the students are required to develop critical thinking capabilities and clear observation and analysis skills for selecting the right set of tools and commands in coding. Focusing on this aspect, the third experiment (Videos) was given to students from two groups and tips and examples were given on how to identify the positive and negative aspects of the videos.

D. Evaluating the outcomes from the experiments

Evaluating actions is one of the most important tasks that can be used to identify if the planned improvement has a positive impact in addressing the problems identified. The first experiment was evaluated during the practical sessions of a class using formative assessment by asking the students there to build a simple HTML form and send messages using GET and POST functions. Interestingly, most of the students were active, engaged and completed the task within the given time and this was compared to students from a previous semester who were not exposed to these Active Learning techniques. 28 students out of 30, completed the task successfully compared to the 19 students who successfully completed the same task in previous year, reflecting a significant improvement in the learning process.

The second experiment (the Jigsaw Technique for algorithmic routing) was evaluated by asking the students to design UML activity diagrams and a flowchart to solve the given real-life problem. The students were found to be effective in adopting the concepts of simplifying complex problems into simpler issues by breaking them down. This was then reflected in their design diagrams and an improvement in their computational skills was observed in designing a flowchart for a real-life problem. Interestingly, all 30 students were able to effectively design the UML diagrams and flowcharts. Only 16 students in the previous year were able to complete this task successfully. The results indicated that collective efforts of the students through discussions, knowledge sharing, team management etc. were found to be significant in solving the problems, leading to the overall development of students.

The third experiment (Videos) was evaluated by asking students to create a group work plan and a Gantt chart for their group assignment. Almost all of the students effectively categorized and identified the tasks for the group work and systematically created a work plan, which was effective and easy to implement. Almost 26 students clearly identified the activities/steps involved with appropriate time schedule for each activity. The results indicate the improvement in the planning, assessment and project management skills of the students, where they need to identify all the relevant tasks, activities, risks, and plan the project/assignment.

E. Planning an Improvement

Overall, the three experiments based on the Active Learning concepts were found to have a positive impact on enhancing the student experiences in using programming languages and their computational thinking. Considering the outcomes of the experiments, these Active Learning techniques are now planned to be used in future teaching of Web Development concepts classes.

III. RESEARCH CHALLENGES AND LIMITATIONS

One of the major challenges identified was about identifying issues or problems associated with the students. The students in the Web Development module were diverse coming from different nations, cultures, and with different experiences and skillsets. While some students had job experience, others did not. So, identifying the differences and getting all of them on a single platform was a big challenge, which was addressed by using a questionnaire-based survey. Other challenges included identifying a suitable pedagogical approach, common interests of students with the type of new learning methods, and their expectations associated with the individual style of teaching being delivered. These issues were addressed by collecting the responses through surveys and discussions, and deciding mutually for using Active Learning techniques as the solution for addressing the identified problem.

IV. CONCLUSION AND FUTURE WORK

Action Research was used for addressing the problem of students with varying skillsets and experiences in understanding the concepts of a Web Development module using Active Learning techniques was the main idea behind this work. Using Active Learning techniques especially the Jigsaw Puzzle have given positive results, and this experiment has led the way forward for introducing new pedagogical approaches in teaching. Finally, this approach could be used continuously to identify changing issues and problems and addressing them using this most effective method of learning and teaching.

REFERENCES

[1] J. M. Hashey and D. J. Connors, “Learning from our journey: Reciprocal teaching action research”. The Reading Teacher, 57, (3), 224–232, 2003.

[2] D. J. Short and J., Echevaria, “The sheltered instruction observation protocol: A tool for teacher-researcher collaboration and professional development”. (EDO-FL-ii-09) Reston, VA: ERIC Clearinghouse on Languages and Linguistics, 1999.

[3] M. Lodico, D. Spaulding and K. Voegtle, Methods in Educational Research. Jossey-Bass Publishers: San Francisco, 2006.

[4] C. J., Brame, “Effective educational videos”. [online] Available at: http://cft.vanderbilt.edu/guides-sub-pages/effective-educational-videos/ [Retrieved: May 2018]

[5] W.L. Byrne, “Four steps to conducting Action Research in the classroom.” [online] Available at: https://wiobyrne.com/action-research/ [Retrieved: May 2018]

[6] A. W. Chickering, and F. G. Zelda, "Seven Principles for Good Practice." AAHE Bulletin 39: 3-7. ED 282 491. 6 pp. 3-7, 1987.

[7] L. M. Duenas, M. A. Rodríguez, J. H. Llopis, “The Jigsaw: A Cooperative Learning Technique As A Tool Of Teaching-Learning Facilitator In Physical Therapy. Effects Of Working With Music As A Motivational Tool To Enhance The Jigsaw Benefits”, EDULEARN14 Proceedings, pp. 3958-3962, 2014.

[8] E. Ferrance, “Themes in Education: Action Research”, Published by Northeast and Islands Regional Educational Laboratory At Brown University, 2000.

[9] L. Fiorella, and R. Mayer, “The relative benefits of learning by teaching and teaching expectancy”. Contemporary Educational Psychology, 38(4), pp.281-288, 2013.

[10] S. Freeman et al.. “Active learning increases student performance in science, engineering, and mathematics”. Proceedings of the National Academy of Sciences, 111(23), 8410-8415, 2014.

[11] R. R. Hake, “Interactive-engagement versus traditional methods: A six-thousand-student survey of mechanics test data for introductory physics courses”. American journal of Physics, 66(1), 64-74, 1998.

[12] V. Hoogerheide, L. Deijkers, S. Loyens, A. Heijltjes and T. van Gog, “Gaining from explaining: Learning improves from explaining to fictitious others on video, not from writing to them”. Contemporary Educational Psychology, 44-45, pp.95-106, 2016.

[13] Indiana University Bloomington, “Effectively Using Videos in the College Classroom”. [online] Available at: https://citl.indiana.edu/teaching-resources/teaching-strategies/effectively-using-video-teaching/ [Accessed: May 2018].

[14] ITLI (Institute for Teaching and Learning Innovation), (2017), "Jigsaw Technique". The University of Queensland. [online]. Available at: http://www.uq.edu.au/teach/flipped-classroom/docs/FAB/FABJigsaw_Tipsheet.pdf [Retrieved: May 2018]

[15] D. W. Johnson and R. T. Johnson, "An educational psychology success story: Social interdependence theory and cooperative learning". Educational Researcher, 38 (5), 365-379, 2009. DOI: 10.3102/0013189X09339057

[16] C. Luo, "An Action Research Plan for Developing and Implementing", The Students' Listening Comprehension Skills.Vol. 1, No. 1. English Language Teaching, 2008.

[17] W. J. McKeachie et al., "Teaching and Learning in the College Classroom: A Review of the Research Literature". Ann Arbor: Regents of The Univ. of Michigan. ED 314 999. 124 pp. MF-01; PC-05, 1986.

[18] J. G. Penner, "Why Many College Teachers Cannot Lecture". Springfield, Ill.: Charles C. Thomas, 1984.

[19] K. L. Ruhl, A. H. Charles, and J. S. Patrick "Using the Pause Procedure to Enhance Lecture Recall." Teacher Education and Special Education 10: 14-18, 1987.

[20] P. Silapachote and A, Srisuphab, "Teaching and learning computational thinking through solving problems in Artificial Intelligence: On designing introductory engineering and computing courses". IEEE International Conference on Teaching, Assessment, and Learning for Engineering (TALE), 2016.

[21] C. Sykora, "Computational thinking for all". [online] Iste.org. Available at: https://www.iste.org/explore/articleDetail?articleid=152 [Retrieved: May 2018].

[22] D. Tripp, "Action research: a methodological introduction ". Education and Research, 31(3), pp.443-466, 2005.

[23] H. Watts, "When teachers are researchers, teaching improves". Journal of Staff Development, 6 (2), 118-127, 1985.

[24] J. M. Wing, "Computational Thinking". [online] Communications of the ACM. Available at: https://www.cs.cmu.edu/~15110-s13/Wing06-ct.pdf [Retrieved: May 2018].

[25] Z. Woolfit, "The effective use of video in higher education". Lectoraat Teaching, Learning and Technology Inholland University of Applied Sciences, 2015.

[26] E. J. Zuckerman, "Videos in Teaching". Augusta University. [online] Available at: http://hdl.handle.net/10675.2/621200 [Retrieved: May 2018]

[27] G.L. Anderson, K. Herr, & L.S. Nihlen, "Studying your own school: An educator's guide to quality practitioner research." Thousand Oaks, CA: Corwin Press, 1994.

[28] J. Creswell. "Mixed-method research: Introduction and application." In C. J. Cizek (Ed.), Handbook of educational policy (pp. 455–472). San Diego: Academic Press, 1999.

[29] U. Zoller, "Scaling-up of higher-order cognitive skills-oriented college chemistry teaching: An action-oriented research", Journal of Research in Science Teaching, vol. 36, no. 5, pp. 583-596, 1999. Available: 10.1002/(sici)1098-2736(199905)36:5<583::aid-tea5>3.0.co;2-m [Accessed 31 January 2019].

[30] D. Mudaly and V. Jugoo, "The use of Action Research in a computer programming module thaught using a blended learning environment ", PONTE International Scientific Researchs Journal, vol. 72, no. 9, 2016. Available: 10.21506/j.ponte.2016.9.5 [Accessed 31 January 2019].

[31] F. Margaret, "Reflecting on my Teaching and Learning in Higher Education". [online] Available at: http://www.actionresearch.net/living/farren/ch6.pdf [Accessed: Jan 2019]

[32] G. Jamwal, "Effective use of interactive learning modules in classroom study in computer science ". [online] Available at: https://digitalcommons.usu.edu/cgi/viewcontent.cgi?article=1223&context=gradreports [Retrieved: Jan 2019]

E-learning Framework for Saudi Universities

Abdullah Salem Alqahtani
School of Information Systems
Curtin University, Perth, Australia
Email: abdullah.alqahtani1@postgrad.curtin.edu.au

Abstract-The emergence of Information and Communication Technologies (ICT) in teaching and learning has brought significant changes in the educational settings of students and teachers. The usage of E-learning in the Kingdom of Saudi Arabia (KSA) academic institutions is still in its early stage and its impact is insignificant. In Saudi Arabian universities, there is a need to improve the understanding of how to deal with the new technology, how to meet the staff and students requirements for teaching and learning, and how to tackle students' lack of motivation concerning independent learning. Hence, this study aims to identify the main issues that are hindering the use of modern techniques of E-learning in Saudi Arabian educational system effectively, such as personal factor, and learning attributes. This study provides an initial framework that can be used as a detailed, structured E-learning roadmap by stakeholders in Saudi universities, as well as those in developing countries. A mixed-methods approach (an explanatory sequential design) will be carried out in Saudi Arabian universities. This study is part of research project and it is anticipated that the findings will increase the awareness of the use and effectiveness of E-learning systems in Saudi's higher education sector.

Keywords-E-learning; Saudi higher education; Initial framework.

I. INTRODUCTION

The education system in the KSA has developed to make sure that education becomes more effective, meets the country's religious, economic and social needs, and eliminates illiteracy among the Saudi youth. The KSA is one of the countries in the world spending the largest amount on education according to the 2014 National Budget. The education and healthcare sectors remain the priority sectors in the national budget. The education sector accounts for 25% of the total expenditure in the national budget and is considered the highest in the world [1]. The KSA has been expected to be one of the fastest developing countries in the world, particularly in establishing E-learning systems in the educational institutions. According to the Information and Communication Technology (CITC 2011), the number of internet users increased rapidly from 200,000 in 2000 to 11,400,000 in 2011, which accounts for 43.6% of the total population [2]. For this reason, Saudi's government has established a new vision and strategy to develop education systems. In particular, the plan is for the public universities in this country to be among the most advanced in the world by 2030. By the year 2030, the government aims to have at least five Saudi universities among the top 200 universities in the international rankings [3]. Currently, the KSA has twenty-six public universities and ten private universities located in various geographic regions. Hamdan [4] and Alharbi [3] pointed out that the Saudi government strives to overcome the challenges the universities encounter such as improving education quality, productivity, accreditation, and develop modern curriculum using different technologies to increase the interaction between teachers and students and focus on the rigorous development of standards in literacy, numeracy, skills, and character. A few studies from the Saudi Arabia perspective [5]-[7] have examined academics' perceptions of E-learning in Saudi higher education. Their findings showed that academics' perceptions toward E-learning integration in their teaching and learning are highly influenced by demographic factors such as age, gender, and education level. Female faculty members perceived less E-learning barriers and they displayed more willingness to implement it while compared to male equivalents.

In line with the aim of this study, an initial framework proposed to measure academics' and students' attitudes toward the effectiveness of E-learning usage in Saudi universities. This paper is organized as following: Section II introduces the current literature relating to E-learning in Saudi education system. Section III describes the research methods. Section IV outlines the research outcomes followed by an initial framework in Section V. The paper concludes the study and scopes future work in Section VI.

II. LITERATURE REVIEW

This paper reviews the current literature relating to E-learning in overall and in the KSA in specific.

A. *E-learning definition*

Dublin [8] and Rosenberg [9] mentioned that the literature on E-learning is vast, which makes it difficult to have a consensual definition of E-learning. In fact, there is no prevalent definition of E-learning. E-learning implies the use of ICT in various processes of education to enhance the learning and teaching, and it offers flexibility in terms of when, how and where information is received and delivered by staff and students [10]. In the context of this study, E-learning has been used in various ways in education. For instance, there is blended learning, online distance learning, and distributed learning. The E-learning environments offer a really interactive and engaging learning approach using various technological tools that are available today such as a whiteboard, video conferencing, audio chatting, online discussion, and Blackboard [11][12]. These technologies give students, academics, and other learners the opportunity to engage in an effective and flexible interaction.

B. *Saudi education system*

The education system in the KSA has developed within the last decade due to the increased population, and the high demand to provide additional instructional opportunities for students. According to [3], the total population of the KSA in 2016 was 32,430,000, which means that most of the population ranges in age from 15 to 64 years. In addition, to meet the increased student enrolment, the number of Saudi public universities has now increased to twenty–six. However, more than 60,000 students are still unable to study in the Saudi public universities because they are already filled to capacity [3]. Furthermore, because of the socio-economic conditions and increased population demands, more students are enrolling in universities and undertaking online learning or are studying overseas [3][13]. Alharbi [3] concluded that the performance of universities, outcomes of quality, and reputation need to be considered by university leaders and face these challenges throughout adopt a benchmark strategy. Therefore, the KSA in 2008 planned to adopt Information and Communication-based Technologies such as E-learning and distance learning in higher education. The mission of the Ministry of Education in the KSA, E-learning not only adds value to and simplifies the traditional education system, but it also improves the quality of education. It develops an environment that incorporates various components of the educational process, thereby not only providing a huge amount of information, but also helping to improve the quality of the education materials [2].

C. *E-learning in Saudi higher education*

Unnisa [1] reported that there are many reasons for the increase in the growth of E-learning in the KSA. First, E-learning has been suggested as a means of overcoming the increasing demand for higher education and solving the problems the universities face with the traditional delivery of education such the overcrowding, lack of facilities, and inadequate human resources. Second, since the KSA is one of a few large countries in the world in terms of its geographical area, and there are a number of communities distant from the major centres of population [14][15], the online E-learning system can provide education facilities to the remote areas without students having to travel to the main location, thereby reducing the geographical inequity. Third, the KSA has a different culture and religion. Especially in the universities, due to religious reasons, the female students study in isolation from the male students. Due to limited facilities and human resource available, it is easier for female students to access higher education via an E-learning system. Currently, E-learning enables course content to be conveyed to students, enabling them to access information and communicate with their teachers easily wherever and whenever they want [16].

D. *National Centre of E-learning and Distance learning (NCEL)*

In 2005, the Ministry of Education in the KSA established the National Centre of E-learning and Distance learning (NCEL) to assist the universities to develop information technology using E-learning [14]. The vision of the NCEL is to implement the techniques of E-learning in the education system, which will improve both learning and teaching outcomes. The NCEL strives to become a national reference for E-learning. Also, one of NCEL's projects is the Saudi Digital Library [17], which holds 310,000 e-books on diverse subjects from 300 international publishers [17].

E. *Student's attitude toward E-learning*

Al-Harbi [15] stated that E-learning success is affected by various factors. A student's attitude toward E-learning is the significant factor in determining a student's intention to utilise the E-learning facilities. Hence, the shaping of the students' behavioural intention about using the E-learning plays a critical role in perceived E-learning success. In the context of the KSA, a study conducted by Al Zumor, et al. [18] shows the impact of students' E-learning acceptance through the Blackboard at King Khalid University. They found that students are willing to use E-learning and accept technology. Similarly, Al-Dosari [7] revealed that academics' and students' attitudes were positive toward using E-learning in the department of English at King Khalid University and the educational system improved as a result of the E-learning environment compared with the traditional learning system. Quadri, Muhammed, Sanober, Qureshi and Shah [19] emphasised that the necessity of E-learning system is more prominent because of the gender-based educational system. Consequently, the E-learning system in Saudi Arabia offers equal opportunity to people seeking education regardless of their gender. In addition, there is a high demand from students who are working in part-time jobs and wish to continue their studies for better opportunities in the future. After inclusive review on the literature related to issues towards the use of E-learning, this study leads to uncovering the E-Learning influential factors that will be critical for understanding the basis of the effectiveness of E-Learning and its impact in Saudi higher educational system.

III. RESEARCH METHODS

To find out the most factors that may influence the effectiveness of E-learning implementation at Saudi higher education, a mixed method will be employed. Mingers [20] has defined the research methodology as the activities and guidelines that assist a researcher to obtain valid and reliable research findings. Silverman [21] agreed with this, and indicated that the research methodology helps a researcher to choose the appropriate research strategy, and data collection techniques, etc. in planning and executing a research study. Hence, Information Systems (IS) researchers frequently encounter challenges in obtaining adequate results and theories that offer fundamental thoughts into a phenomenon of interest [22].

A. *Pragmatism philosophy*

The philosophy of this research is pragmatism with an abductive approach to determine the use of E-learning systems in Saudi higher education and then generate an initial framework [23]. Pragmatism philosophy was proposed for IS researchers. They advocate the use of mixed methodologies as one of the favored paradigms for amending the usage of mixed-methods research [22]. In this paper, the research method is the mixed-methods design to achieve the research aims and answer the research questions by using Explanatory Sequential Design. This means that the data will be gathered equally through a quantitative approach using an online survey and a qualitative approach using semi-structured interviews to understand the research problem, then the data from each approach is analysed separately and then merged into one study [24][25].

Venkatesh et al. [22] stated that if the Information Systems researcher decides to conduct a research for which a powerful theoretical basis previously exists. However, if the study context is novel or past results were unsatisfactory or indecisive, the researcher should take into account using a quantitative approach first, followed by a qualitative approach to offer further insights based upon the context-specified results. This research methodology is adopted based on the understanding of the study objective that can be delivered by the quantitative approach and the subsequent data analysis. In the qualitative phase, Creswell et al. [26] mentioned that the statistical findings for participants' views will be processed and clarified by means of interviews. This research will use the mixed-methods approach to offer a general understanding regarding the use of E-learning systems in Saudi higher education.

In the first phase, this research will investigate the academics' and students' attitudes toward using E-learning systems in Saudi higher education through a quantitative (deductive) approach to understand their reactions to using E-learning systems and to develop a range of new factors from the survey [27]. The online survey will be used to examine the five factors that may influence the use of E-learning. In the second phase, a qualitative (inductive) approach will be conducted with the help of semi-structured interviews to analyse the data in depth and to obtain an understanding of the phenomena in its real-life context and through the meanings that people assign to them. The validity and reliability of mixed methods research are achieved by fundamentally measuring the quality of results or deductions from all of the quantitative and qualitative data in the research inquiry [22]. Tashakkori and Creswell [28] report that the surveys in a quantitative data gathering approach can bring breadth to a research by assisting researchers to collect data about various aspects of a phenomenon from many participants. Subsequently, the validation of the qualitative data collection will be used by conducting the interviews to provide the depth in the research inquiry and allow the researcher to obtain deep insights from rich data.

For the purpose of this study, the researcher will also use the quantitative data to determine the factors that may influence the use of E-learning systems in Saudi higher education followed by a qualitative approach so as to understand academics' attitudes toward the use of E-learning systems. In this regard, the factor analysis will be applied to achieve a rigorous picture of what might create a successful set of factors for a framework for E-learning within the context under examination. Hence, the factor analysis technique can be used to reduce data by grouping it into factors. According to Pallant [29], factor analysis has been used as a compression methodology that manages a large set of factors by decreasing it based on correlations that exist between variables, and can then be utilized in other tests.

B. *The participants*

The participant population for this research will include all academics and students who are currently enrolled in Saudi universities. In order to obtain valuable results, three public universities will be selected to identify the factors influencing the E-learning systems in Saudi higher education.

C. *Quantitative online survey*

In the first phase, quantitative data will be used to examine the factors that will ensure the effectiveness of E-learning in the Saudi higher education framework and to identify the factors for the proposed framework. Consequently, an online survey utilising Qualtrics software will be distributed via E-mail to all participants (academics and students). Data analysis will be conducted using IBM SPSS (version 25) statistics, and exploratory factor analysis (EFA) will be applied for statistical testing of the gathered data to identify the factors for the proposed framework for the E-learning usage in Saudi higher education.

D. *Qualitative interviewing*

In the second phase, semi-structured questionnaire will be conducted to collect information regarding the opinions and attitudes of experts toward the use of E-learning systems in Saudi higher education. A suitable strategy for gathering the data is to ask open-ended questions through face-to-face interviews or to use other technological applications such as Skype in order to allow the researcher to explore various opinions of individuals. The sample size of semi-structured interviews in this study will be determined between six to ten interviews. In terms of the upper limits of qualitative sample size, previous Information Systems studies pointed out that there is no recommended number of interviews. Recent studies suggest that the sample size should be 5-10 interviewees so that the researcher ensures that the state of theoretical saturation has occurred [30][32]. A thematic analysis technique will be employed in order to develop themes based on analysing and detecting data and also grouping the information according to identified patterns. Following this grouping of themes, the data will be analysed using NVivo software (version 11) [31][33]. Furthermore, King and Horrocks [34] highlighted interview methods involving connecting elements, recording, interview venue, the introduction and conclusion of the interviews.

IV. RESEARCH OUTCOMES

Numerous studies [1][2][5][6][15][35][36] have been conducted in Saudi Arabia to implement E-learning in the education sector to improve students' learning outcomes. However, none of the articles which have been reviewed identify these factors such as, Technological Pedagogical Content Knowledge (TPACK), ICT factors, teaching principles, learning attributes, and personal factors on the effectiveness of E-learning use. After reviewing these studies, some of the factors were missing in some models, and hence an initial framework will be developed to examine the gap in the literature of a theoretical framework for the effectiveness of E-learning use in teaching and learning especially in Saudi Arabia. Education is the most important sector in any country, especially developing countries like the KSA. Therefore, educational institutions need to extensively use the Information and Communication Technologies as an alternative method of course delivery to students in order to guarantee that technologies are utilized efficiently within education sectors [2]. One of the modern common technologies is E-learning which plays a significant role in developing learning environments. The academics and students are likely to face some problems when adopting E-learning in the Saudi universities such as meeting staff and students requirements for teaching and learning, and the poor understanding of the new technology such as web 2.0 [19]. Currently, the Saudi universities face extensive pressure due to an increase in the number of prospective students and the limited number of places available [37]. Hence, with the opportunity of remote learning being facilitated through the successful incorporation of E-learning into teaching practice, this issue may be mitigated or even resolved. The lectures and lesson times are short in certain subjects such as applied science, medical, and engineering programs offered by faculties in Saudi universities. So, the provision of E-learning in these faculties will provide various teaching methods involving the computerised methods of blended learning practices which can help to address this issue [18].

The lack of knowledge in the use of technologies, and the underdeveloped university websites need to improve in updating their information and presenting the information in a usable manner to the students and academics, and offering training programs to help staff design their modules. ICT infrastructure is one of the biggest challenges in the implementation of E-learning in the higher education sector due to interruption problems with the internet. Furthermore, the KSA has a different culture because the delivery of education is segregated according to gender as it is not permitted for the male lecturer to teach female students face-to-face according to Islamic law [15][37][38]. KSA is one of the most conservative Muslim countries in the world, particularly regarding the situation of women, and it has solid roots in religious and family histories compared to developing countries [39][42]. For this reason, E-learning could help to solve this issue as male lecturers can teach female students through Blackboard or video-conferences by using such technologies.

Moreover, gender is a significant factor and believed to be of influence on academics' attitudes toward E-learning implementation [6]. Consequently, female faculty members held more positive attitudes toward E-learning integration in teaching and learning compared to their male counterparts [5][7]. However, to the best of the researcher's knowledge, none of the previous literature yet has examined all of these factors inclusively, such as TPACK, ICT factors, teaching principles, learning attributes, and personal factors. These factors have been chosen as they are the most prominent in existing E-learning literature.

V. E-LEARNING INITIAL FRAMEWORK

The proposed framework in this research is designed to integrate a set of the influential factors drawn from existing literature which must be considered when addressing E-learning systems in Saudi's higher education as well as achieving the research aims. It consists of five factors: TPACK, ICT factors, teaching principles, learning attributes, and personal factors (see Figure 1).

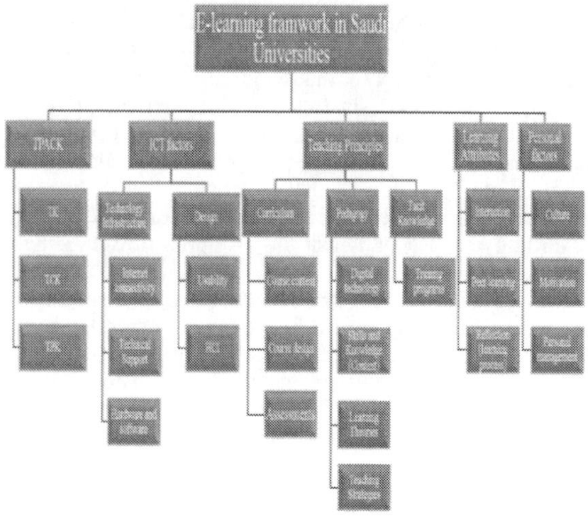

Figure 1: E-learning Framework in Saudi Universities

A. Technological Pedagogical Content Knowledge (TPACK)

A few decades ago, Shulman [43] developed the concept of Pedagogical Content Knowledge (PCK), combining the relationships between content knowledge that the academics view as the need to teach subject matter separately from the way it needs to be taught, and the technological knowledge that refers to knowledge of E-learning such as the Internet, digital video, blackboards etc. Twenty years later, Mishra and Koehler [44] integrated the third domain and created the technology-based conceptual framework proposed by Shulman (PCK-TPACK) framework to become the Technological Pedagogical and Content Knowledge (TPACK). TPACK defines as, a framework that is used to include an understanding of the complexity of the relationships between academics, students, content, technologies such as (E-learning), practices, and tools [45]. Also, TPACK describes teacher knowledge for the technology integration into the learning environment. Niess [46] indicates that the TPACK framework develops academics' knowledge of subject content using technology such as E-learning to facilitate student learning and pedagogical knowledge.

Mishra and Koehler [44] noted that TPACK is the integrated forms of knowledge that develop the interaction between these three main forms, namely, Technological Pedagogical Knowledge (TPK) that encourages interactivity among students in E-learning and the understanding of how E-learning can influence learning and teaching, and the Technological Content Knowledge (TCK) that the academics use in E-learning to enhance students' skills and understanding of the concepts in a specific subject matter, and Pedagogical Content Knowledge (PCK) [14][47][48].

In this study, the researcher focuses on the type of knowledge that include technology (E-learning) such as TK, TPK, TCK, TPACK since these are directly related to the study objectives. A study was conducted by Habowski and Mouza [47] to investigate the use of technology for pre-service science teachers in a Mid-Atlantic University in the USA. They found that the pre-service teachers had opportunities to integrate content, pedagogy, and technology in their practice. They used online resources such as YouTube video clips to present topics in biology and physics. Habowski and Mouza [47] used the survey of TPACK framework to measure pre-service teachers' knowledge and technology in science, and their findings show that pre-service teachers' TPK documents more than their TCK. Similarity, a study conducted on pre-service elementary teachers [49] through open-ended pre-service teachers' responses found that out of 55 teachers, 22 agreed with TPK compared with TCK. Evidently, the TPACK framework could be used as a determinant to measure the extent to which academics actually use E-learning in their educational practice. Also, the results could provide better ways to prepare pre-service teachers for the integration of E-learning in education [50].

B. *ICT Factors*

According to Kabilan and Rajab [51] and Al-Adwan and Smedley [10], ICT infrastructures can be used in teaching and learning environments. Implementation of ICT in teaching and learning is challenging not only for the students, academics and instructional materials but also for the teachers'/lecturers' awareness, acceptance, technical and skills. A suitable infrastructure for ICT development such as the availability of the internet, extranet, intranet and LAN networks is also necessary for the implementation of E-learning in higher education, especially in developing countries [10][11]. Hence, dealing with the challenges in the implementation of E-learning is important. In the Saudi higher education system, Altameem [52] revealed that some technical constraints in several universities such as inadequate ICT infrastructures preventing the successful development and implementation of E-learning systems. For example, the lack of the availability of the internet facility at any time, and the inadequate bandwidths hamper the academics' teaching and the students' learning when there is access. Mokhtar, Alias and Rahman [53] suggest that the lack of resources and ICT equipment such as software and hardware especially those related to computers, teaching-learning materials and classroom size [54], shortcomings in teacher development [55], and lack of online IT support [11] made teachers less inclined to implement the online-based teaching and learning methods. Also, a critical factor recognized by the students is that more attention needed to be paid by Saudi universities to this aspect of E-learning [52]. Moreover, higher education institutions must invest in the right ICT infrastructure that allows academics and students to readily access the ICT hardware, utilizing friendly software and offering permanent technical support [10].

Another ICT factor in this research is the usability of the developed software which is easy to use [56]. Usability is the main consideration when developing E-learning technology, as it is also for other kinds of software since usability helps to develop the systems with improved instructional and pedagogical approaches. According to Juristo, Lopez, Moreno and Sánchez [56], usability is often ignored in the design of E-learning software. Bevan and Azuma [57] mentioned that usability means that the software is simple to learn, effective to use, easy to remember, has few errors, and is subjectively satisfactory, [58] as well having performance, acceptance, and learnability. Additionally, web usability is becoming a significant issue for E-learning and an important factor in the planning and use of E-learning applications. Battleson, Booth and Weintrop [59] considered usability as a component of Human-Computer Interaction (HCI); it is defined as "the ease with which a user can learn to operate, prepare inputs for, and interpret outputs of a system or component" [60]. Hence, HCI is about the interaction between computers and users [61]. However, an E-learning system that aligns with students' and academics' needs is desirable and more useful. Obviously, lecturers and students should be involved in the HCI development process in order for their reactions and other behavioural factors to be taken into account at the time they use the computer [62]. Therefore, as many Saudi universities have introduced E-learning systems, the current study aims to help the universities in the KSA in their endeavour to successfully use E-learning systems by discovering the key challenges such as ICT infrastructure, Internet connectivity, technical support, usability and Human-Computer Interaction (HCI) that enable the academics and students to use E-learning effectively.

C. *Teaching principles*

The traditional curriculum design is such that the academics focus on the content delivery and on the assessment by means of which the students' knowledge and absorption of the taught material can be ascertained. Tam [63] reported that the curriculum designers and academics reflect through planning what should be learned, and select the learning activities appropriate for the desired outcomes. They are required to create and develop the learning environments not only for the academics to be proficient in their discipline but also for the use of a diversity of resources, methods, technologies. These include the E-learning systems, assessment resources, and e-mail so that the students achieve valuable outcomes. The academics need to change their role from the subject- proficient teacher to being facilitators of the learning process. Through this, the learning and teaching activities will be aligned with the educational process instead of being just content-driven [63]. The focus on learning requires the academics to develop the syllabus [64], and establish a course syllabus which becomes a central for documentation and demonstration of curriculum intentions [65]. Syllabi can make particular course outcomes clear in the context of broader program outcomes and can direct the students to work when the assignments are due and identify the kind and level of anticipations, and what are the aims that will be reached [65]. In regards to using E-learning in higher education, Meyen, et al. [66] stated that the pedagogy of online teaching involves "teaching methods related to the presentation of experiences, engagement of learners, reinforcement, motivation, an organization of teaching tasks, feedback, evolution, and curriculum integration" (2002, 40).

Another study by Dron [67] mentioned that pedagogies are, in a true and essential sense, the area of study relating to teaching and as a strategy for education; and technologies represent a series of techniques and tools for education. For instance, technologies involve the use of computers, discussion boards, virtual classrooms, and institutional constructions. Hence, the adoption or acceptance of new technologies (like E-learning) needs to create pedagogical concepts that could not be applied without technology and considers the current and future needs of the students, which are essential in a digital world. To use new technologies and create digital pedagogies, we need to know what to use, how to use, and when, and for what purpose. In the education field, the academics and students have access to the internet. So, there is a need to change their knowledge about using the technology so that it is more useful.

Lawless and Pellegrino [68] and Dron [67] pointed out that knowledge sharing has become more significant than the knowledge itself. Therefore, creating digital pedagogies will shift the concentration from technology and skills to one that consists of connectivity, knowledge process, interaction, and development of knowledge by working in the digital world. Palomba and Banta [69] indicated that the academics deliver course content to students by determining what should be learned in order to achieve the desired learning outcomes; and whether their expected learning outcomes are introduced and reinforced in the given educational course. In the same context, Biggs [70] pointed out that the learning outcomes, the teaching and learning activities should be aligned, and this is determined by the assessment system. The alignment of these three components will ensure the coherence in the curriculum in terms of the desired learning outcomes which should correspond with the teaching and learning activities, and the assessment tasks should be consistent [63][70]. However, in the case of the Saudi higher education system, Saudi vision 2030 wants the academics to have effective training and academic processing for teaching online courses in order to improve the teaching curriculum and enhance the E-learning systems in all subjects [3][71].

D. *Learning Attributes*

Maor [72] stated that the learning attributes were utilized as the basis for the students' perception of the courses and the students' interaction. For more explanation, Interaction means that students share knowledge and interact with their peers and teachers by using discussion boards. Peer learning refers to students reflecting on the comments made during peer conversations on and offline. Reflection practice means that students create reflective journals by using technology such as Blackboards to show their understanding and transformation in their thinking over time. For instance, reflection refers to the learning process that assists students to express their attitudes, feelings, experiences, actions, and beliefs. It provides students with opportunities to examine the knowledge they have absorbed [73]. The interaction between the lecturer and students enables the lecturer to pose questions to encourage students to engage in reflective thinking.

In E-learning environments, the term 'interaction' could refer to learning activities and includes the online communication between lecturers and students, sharing information, and exchanging learning experiences. There are various types of interactions such as learning content interaction, student-student communication, and student-lecturer communication [74]. In an E-learning, students engage in interpersonal interaction over computer networks and interfaces instead of face-to-face communication. The synchronous communication or interaction may occur online between students and lecturers, and among students in E-learning environments, and may involve questions, answers, and discussions [75].

In previous studies, the interaction between students and lecturers means that lecturers must perform a variety of tasks in the process of teaching such as providing an overview of the course contents, giving feedback on achievements, stimulating students' motivation to process and reflect on the content, and helping them to engage in learning activities, supporting knowledge construction, and establishing the foundation for a social relationship [74][76]. Students' peer interactions comprise the communication processes among the students, where students exchange information about the course contents and socio-emotional information. Students benefit from working in small groups to construct understanding, provide socio-emotional support, and learn within a consistent and positive environment [75][77]. According to Wong and Bakar [78], the interactive learning environment is an important factor in promoting students' positive attitudes through perceived satisfaction, usefulness, and peer learning, and reflect students' skills required for problem-solving in the E-learning environment [74].

E. *Personal Factors*

Al-Adwan and Smedley [10] reported that any institution wants to have a successful E-learning strategy should be prepared culturally as well technologically. Cultural factors have a massive influence on how students learn, involving the style of interaction and communication, establishing the core basis of E-learning. These factors strongly impact two key elements of online learning systems: 1) system development and design, and 2) system usability and usage [79]. Hence, the engagement of cultural characteristics of academics and students is an important motivational factor in designing E-learning system and in contributing to the acceleration of the usage process toward the technology [80]. However, the KSA has a different religious and cultural influence on people's attitudes, practices, and behaviour [14]. Also, their social life and living standards are different and this may influence the success of the E-learning in higher education [19].

Baki [39] notes that the Saudi system and methods of education differ from those of other countries around the world due to the different culture and religious beliefs. Asiri [44] agreed with him as the KSA is one of the most conservative Muslim countries in the world, particularly regarding the situation of women. In the KSA, male and female students in the universities are completely segregated. Consequently, the male academics cannot teach female students to face-to-face due to the Islamic restriction imposed by the Saudi government. The faculty members provide lectures to female students separately in buildings equipped with the audio-visual materials. This puts a substantial pressure on the available resources and facilities [41]. Therefore, Saudi universities are encouraged to introduce E-learning system to offer online courses for the female students in different faculties via a variety of E-learning systems [15][19].

Another study conducted by Hussein [81] investigated the attitudes of Saudi universities' faculty members towards using the learning management system (JUSUR). His findings show that 85% of the participants have a positive attitude towards the E-learning management system JUSUR, and no variances in the attitudes among the faculty members regarding gender or the college classification type, whether it be the humanities, sciences or health subjects. In addition, the research results demonstrate that the faculty members have sufficient awareness of the significance of E-learning and usage of technology in teaching. This indicates a significant encouraging sign for the development of the use of E-learning management systems by faculty members [82]. However, Hussein [81] suggests some weakness in the activation of E-learning management systems based on the participants' responses: the shortage of awareness regarding the basics of using the E-learning system; concerns of some faculty members and students' families regarding the E-learning; and the resistance of the community to the E-learning systems as they consider that technology is for entertainment, not for learning.

Yahya et al. [83] indicated that personal management is the different needs and preferences of learner which involves the learning style and technical skills needed to solve the problems that occur when the learner access the E-learning system. Personal management means that academics become more knowledgeable about the technology that they use in the classroom. Academics must overcome personal confusion and uncertainty through being aware of the issues that they face such as time management of non-academic problems related to technology and thereby helping IT developers recognize their academics needs and providing them easily [84].

VI. CONCLUSION AND FUTURE WORK

As a conclusion, the main purpose of this research is to develop the awareness of academics and students regarding the use of E-learning technology in Saudi higher education. This research is expected to have a practical implication. To the best of the researcher's knowledge, none of the previous literature yet has examined all provided factors in the proposed framework inclusively. The deliverable outcome of this research will be a framework that provides a clearly structured roadmap for the stakeholders to use E-learning within the Saudi universities and it can be carried out in those developing countries especially, the Gulf Cooperation Council (GCC) countries due to they share the same factors such as culture, languages, religion, and education system. Centred on the university level, it is anticipated that the findings will enlighten stakeholders about the different uses of E-learning, and how these can be encouraged to develop learning and teaching at the university itself, and in the KSA higher education sector in general.

In future work, we plan to extend current research by investigating the influential factors on the effectiveness of E-learning usage in Saudi universities and its impact on student learning outcomes. In addition, this paper is part of a broader research project and the findings will be utilized as the basis of an in-depth survey which will be published in future research.

REFERENCES

[1] S. Unnisa, "E-Learning in Saudi Arabia's Higher Education," Kuwait Chapter of the Arabian Journal of Business and Management Review, vol. 4, no. 2, pp. 152-157, 2014.

[2] S. Alkhalaf, S. Drew, R. AlGhamdi, and O. Alfarraj, "E-Learning system on higher education institutions in KSA: attitudes and perceptions of faculty members," Procedia-Social and Behavioral Sciences, vol. 47, pp. 1199-1205, 2012.

[3] E. A. R. Alharbi, "Higher Education in Saudi Arabia: Challenges to Achieving World-Class Recognition," International Journal of Culture and History, vol. 2, no. 4, pp. 169, 2016.

[4] A. Hamdan, "An Exploration into" Private" Higher Education in Saudi Arabia: Improving Quality and Accessibility?," The ACPET Journal for Private Higher Education, vol. 2, no. 2, pp. 33, 2013.

[5] A. Alenezi, "Faculty members' perception of e-learning in higher education in the Kingdom of Saudi Arabia(KSA)," PhD diss., Texas Tech University, 2012. http://hdl.handle.net/2346/45399

[6] M. Al Gamdi, and A. Samarji, "Perceived barriers towards e-Learning by faculty members at a recently established university in Saudi Arabia," International Journal of Information and Education Technology, vol. 6, no. 1, pp. 23, 2016.

[7] H. Al-Dosari, "Faculty members and students perceptions of e-learning in the English department: A project evaluation," Journal of Social Sciences, vol. 7, no. 3, pp. 291, 2011.

[8] L. Dublin, "If you only look under the street lamps... or nine e-learning myths," Best of The, pp. 1, 2003.

[9] M. J. Rosenberg, E-learning: Strategies for delivering knowledge in the digital age: McGraw-Hill New York, 2001.

[10] A. Al-Adwan, and J. Smedley, "Implementing e-learning in the Jordanian higher education system: Factors affecting impact," International Journal of Education and Development using Information and Communication Technology, vol. 8, no. 1, pp. 121, 2012.

[11] A. Sife, E. Lwoga, and C. Sanga, "New technologies for teaching and learning: Challenges for higher learning institutions in developing countries," International journal of education and development using ICT, vol. 3, no. 2, pp. 57-67, 2007.

[12] S. Guri-Rosenblit, "Distance education in the digital age: Common misconceptions and challenging tasks," Journal of Distance Education (Online), vol. 23, no. 2, pp. 105, 2009.

[13] K. T. Hilal, "Between the fears and hopes for a different future for the nation-states: Scholarship programs in Saudi Arabia and United Arab Emirates from a public policy standpoint," International Journal of Higher Education, vol. 2, no. 2, pp. 195, 2013.

[14] R. Alebaikan, and S. Troudi, "Blended learning in Saudi universities: challenges and perspectives," ALT-J, vol. 18, no. 1, pp. 49-59, 2010.

[15] K. A.-S. Al-Harbi, "E-Learning in the Saudi tertiary education: Potential and challenges," Applied Computing and Informatics, vol. 9, no. 1, pp. 31-46, 2011.

[16] M. Alamri, "Higher education in Saudi Arabia," Journal of Higher Education Theory and Practice, vol. 11, no. 4, pp. 88, 2011.

[17] SDL. "The Saudi Digital Library ", May 12, 2018, https://sdl.edu.sa/SDLPortal/en/Publishers.aspx,

[18] A. W. Q. Al Zumor, I. K. Al Refaai, E. A. B. Eddin, and F. H. A. Al-Rahman, "EFL Students' perceptions of a blended learning environment: Advantages, limitations and suggestions for improvement," English Language Teaching, vol. 6, no. 10, pp. 95, 2013.

[19] N. Quadri, A. Muhammed, S. Sanober, and A. Shah, "Barriers Effecting Successful Implementation of E-Learning in Saudi Arabian Universities," International Journal of Emerging Technologies in Learning (iJET), vol. 12, no. 06, pp. 94-107, 2017.

[20] J. Mingers, "Combining IS research methods: towards a pluralist methodology," Information systems research, vol. 12, no. 3, pp. 240-259, 2001.

[21] D. Silverman, Interpreting qualitative data: Sage, 2015.

[22] V. Venkatesh, S. A. Brown, and H. Bala, "Bridging the qualitative-quantitative divide: Guidelines for conducting mixed methods research in information systems," MIS quarterly, vol. 37, no. 1, pp. 21-54, 2013.

[23] M. Saunders, P. Lewis, and A. Thornhill, "Research Methods for business students 7th edition Pearson education limited," 2016.

[24] J. W. Creswell, A concise introduction to mixed methods research: Sage Publications, 2014.

[25] J. M. Morse, Mixed method design: Principles and procedures: Routledge, 2016.

[26] J. W. Creswell, and V. L. P. Clark, "Designing and conducting mixed methods research,": Sage Publications, 2017.

[27] D. M. Mertens, Research and evaluation in education and psychology: Integrating diversity with quantitative, qualitative, and mixed methods: Sage publications, 2014.

[28] A. Tashakkori, and J. W. Creswell, "Mixed methodology across disciplines," Sage Publications Sage CA: Los Angeles, CA, 2008.

[29] J. Pallant, SPSS survival manual: McGraw-Hill Education (UK), 2013.

[30] B. Marshall et al., "Does sample size matter in qualitative research?: A review of qualitative interviews in IS research," Journal of Computer Information Systems, vol. 54, no. 1, pp. 11-22, 2013.

[31] J. W. Creswell, and C. N. Poth, Qualitative inquiry and research design: Choosing among five approaches: Sage publications, 2017.

[32] R. K. Yin, Case study research: Design and methods: Sage publications, 2013.

[33] J. A. Maxwell, Qualitative research design: An interactive approach: Sage publications, 2012.

[34] N. King, and C. Horrocks, Interviews in qualitative research: Sage, 2010.

[35] A. M. Al-Asmari, and M. S. Rabb Khan, "E-learning in Saudi Arabia: Past, present and future," Near and Middle Eastern Journal of Research in Education, pp. 2, 2014.

[36] F. N. Al-Fahad, "Students attitudes and perceptions towards the effectiveness of mobile learning in King Saud University, Saudi Arabia," Turkish Online Journal of Educational Technology, vol. 8, no. 2, pp. 111-119, 2009.

[37] M. Algahtani, "Factors influencing the adoption of learning management systems in the Kingdom of Saudi Arabian universities by female academic staff," 2017.

[38] A. Onsman, "It is better to light a candle than to ban the darkness: government led academic development in Saudi Arabian universities," Higher Education, vol. 62, no. 4, pp. 519-532, 2011.

[39] R. Baki, "Gender-Segregated Education in Saudi Arabia: Its Impact on Social Norms and the Saudi Labor Market," education policy analysis archives, vol. 12, no. 28, pp. n28, 2004.

[40] S. Almutairy, T. Davies, and Y. Dimitriadi, "The readiness of applying m-learning among Saudi Arabian students at higher education." pp. 102-106.

[41] M. J. S. Asiri, "Factors influencing the use of learning management system in Saudi Arabian Higher Education: A theoretical framework," Higher Education Studies, vol. 2, no. 2, pp. 125-137, 2012.

[42] J. G. Alzahrani, and G. Ghinea, "Evaluating the impact of interactivity issues on e-learning effectiveness." pp. 1-5.

[43] L. S. Shulman, "Paradigms and research programs in the study of teaching: A contemporary perspective," 1986.

[44] P. Mishra, and M. J. Koehler, "Technological pedagogical content knowledge: A framework for teacher knowledge," Teachers college record, vol. 108, no. 6, pp. 1017, 2006.

[45] L. Archambault, "Using TPACK as framework for understanding effective online teaching." pp. 5190-5195.

[46] M. L. Niess, "Preparing teachers to teach science and mathematics with technology: Developing a technology pedagogical content knowledge," Teaching and teacher education, vol. 21, no. 5, pp. 509-523, 2005.

[47] T. Habowski, and C. Mouza, "Pre-service teachers' development of technological pedagogical content knowledge (TPACK) in the context of a secondary science teacher education program," Journal of Technology and Teacher Education, vol. 22, no. 4, pp. 471-495, 2014.

[48] C. S. Chai, J. H. L. Koh, and C.-C. Tsai, "Facilitating preservice teachers' development of technological, pedagogical, and content knowledge (TPACK)," Educational Technology & Society, vol. 13, no. 4, pp. 63-73, 2010.

[49] M. Hofer, and J. Harris, "TPACK research with inservice teachers: Where's the TCK?." pp. 4704-4709.

[50] J. Tondeur et al., "A comprehensive investigation of TPACK within pre-service teachers' ICT profiles: Mind the gap!," Australasian Journal of Educational Technology, vol. 33, no. 3, pp. 46-60, 2017.

[51] M. K. Kabilan, and B. M. Rajab, "The utilisation of the Internet by Palestinian English language teachers focusing on uses, practices and barriers and overall contribution to professional development," International Journal of Education and Development using Information and Communication Technology, vol. 6, no. 3, pp. 56, 2010.

[52] A. Altameem, "What drives successful E-learning? An empirical investigation of the key technical issues in Saudi Arabian universities, " Journal of Theoretical & Applied Information Technology, vol. 53, no. 1, pp. 63-70, 2013.

[53] S. A. Mokhtar, R. A. Alias, and A. A. Rahman, "Academic computing at Malaysian colleges," International Journal of Education and Development using ICT, vol. 3, no. 2, 2007.

[54] P. J. Clarke, "Exploring the use of computer technology in a Caribbean context: Views of preservice teachers," International Journal of Education and Development using ICT, vol. 3, no. 1, 2007.

[55] R. Wells, and S. Wells, "Challenges and opportunities in ICT educational development: A Ugandan case study," international journal of Education and Development using ICT, vol. 3, no. 2, 2007.

[56] N. Juristo et al., "Improving software usability through architectural patterns." pp. 12-19.

[57] N. Bevan, and M. Azuma, "Quality in use: Incorporating human factors into the software engineering lifecycle." pp. 169-179.

[58] K. J. Alotaibi, "Gathering of usability requirements by Saudi e-learning software developers." pp. 255-261.

[59] B. Battleson, A. Booth, and J. Weintrop, "Usability testing of an academic library web site: a case study," The Journal of Academic Librarianship, vol. 27, no. 3, pp. 188-198, 2001.

[60] H. S. Al-Khalifa, "A first step in evaluating the usability of Jusur learning management system." pp. 450-459.

[61] T. Issa, and P. Isaias, "Usability and Human Computer Interaction (HCI)," Sustainable Design, pp. 19-36: Springer, 2015.

[62] A. J. Head, Design wise: A guide for evaluating the interface design of information resources: Information Today, Inc., 1999.

[63] M. Tam, "Outcomes-based approach to quality assessment and curriculum improvement in higher education," Quality Assurance in Education, vol. 22, no. 2, pp. 158-168, 2014.

[64] M. B. Eberly, S. E. Newton, and R. A. Wiggins, "The syllabus as a tool for student-centered learning," The Journal of General Education, vol. 50, no. 1, pp. 56-74, 2001.

[65] N. F. Veltri et al., "Curriculum mapping as a tool for continuous improvement of IS curriculum," Journal of Information Systems Education, vol. 22, no. 1, pp. 31, 2011.

[66] E. L. Meyen et al., "e-Learning: A programmatic research construct for the future," Journal of Special Education Technology, vol. 17, no. 3, pp. 37-46, 2002.

[67] J. Dron, "The pedagogical-technological divide and the elephant in the room," International Journal on E-learning, vol. 11, no. 1, pp. 23-38, 2012.

[68] K. A. Lawless, and J. W. Pellegrino, "Professional development in integrating technology into teaching and learning: Knowns, unknowns, and ways to pursue better questions and answers," Review of educational research, vol. 77, no. 4, pp. 575-614, 2007.

[69] C. A. Palomba, and T. W. Banta, Assessment Essentials: Planning, Implementing, and Improving Assessment in Higher Education. Higher and Adult Education Series: ERIC, 1999.

[70] J. B. Biggs, Teaching for quality learning at university: What the student does: McGraw-Hill Education (UK), 2011.

[71] N. Yusuf, "Changes Required in Saudi Universities Curriculum to Meet the Demands of 2030 Vision," International Journal of Economics and Finance, vol. 9, no. 9, pp. 111, 2017.

[72] D. Maor, "Using TPACK to develop digital pedagogues: a higher education experience," Journal of Computers in Education, vol. 4, no. 1, pp. 71-86, 2017.

[73] S.-W. Hsieh et al., "Effects of teaching and learning styles on students' reflection levels for ubiquitous learning," Computers & Education, vol. 57, no. 1, pp. 1194-1201, 2011.

[74] S.-S. Liaw, and H.-M. Huang, "Perceived satisfaction, perceived usefulness and interactive learning environments as predictors to self-regulation in e-learning environments," Computers & Education, vol. 60, no. 1, pp. 14-24, 2013.

[75] A. N. Islam, "Investigating e-learning system usage outcomes in the university context," Computers & Education, vol. 69, pp. 387-399, 2013.

[76] M. Paechter, B. Maier, and D. Macher, "Students' expectations of, and experiences in e-learning: Their relation to learning achievements and course satisfaction," Computers & education, vol. 54, no. 1, pp. 222-229, 2010.

[77] D. Y. Shee, and Y.-S. Wang, "Multi-criteria evaluation of the web-based e-learning system: A methodology based on learner satisfaction and its applications," Computers & Education, vol. 50, no. 3, pp. 894-905, 2008.

[78] S. L. Wong, and K. A. Bakar, "Qualitative findings of students' perception on practice of self-regulated strategies in online community discussion," Computers & education, vol. 53, no. 1, pp. 94-103, 2009.

[79] A. Rhema, and I. Miliszewska, "Towards e-learning in higher education in Libya," Issues in Informing Science and Information Technology, vol. 7, no. 1, pp. 423-437, 2010.

[80] L. Vrazalic, R. MacGregor, and D. Behl, "E-learning barriers in the United Arab Emirates: Preliminary results from an empirical investigation," IBIMA Business Review, 2010.

[81] H. B. Hussein, "Attitudes of Saudi universities faculty members towards using learning management system (JUSUR)," TOJET: The Turkish Online Journal of Educational Technology, vol. 10, no. 2, 2011.

[82] W. M. Pollock, The impact of on-line training on college faculty attitudes and knowledge of students with disabilities: Old Dominion University, 2009.

[83] M. Al-Yahya, R. George, and A. Alfaries, "Ontologies in E-learning: review of the literature," International Journal of Software Engineering and Its Applications, vol. 9, no. 2, pp. 67-84, 2015.

[84] Y.-H. Chen, and S.-J. Jang, "Interrelationship between stages of concern and technological, pedagogical, and content knowledge: A study on Taiwanese senior high school in-service teachers," Computers in Human Behavior, vol. 32, pp. 79-91, 2014.

Teaching Arabic with Technology Project-Based Learning

A non-traditional approach to summative assessment

Odeese Mariam Ghassa-Khalil
Department of Instructional Technology and Leadership, School of Education
Duquesne University
Pittsburgh, PA, United States
e-mail: GhassaKhalilo@duq.edu

Abstract— **This paper seeks to demonstrate how Technology Project-Based Learning can be applied in the classroom to make learning more enjoyable, interdisciplinary, and applicable to real life. Being experienced in teaching Arabic in the traditional, hybrid, synchronous, and asynchronous online environment, the author shares her perspective on implementing a technology-infused, teacher-facilitated, and student-driven, project-based assessment challenge. She explains how this challenge allows for a higher level of creativity and can be applied to other subject areas. She defines Technology Project-Based Learning as a methodology that enriches the learning environment and complements academic instruction and curricular design. The author then summarizes how the Technology in Technology Project-Based Learning allows for a higher level of creativity in the classroom, in which students' perspectives expand as they prepare to navigate an ever-changing technological world.**

Keywords- Arabic; Learner-Driven, Collaboration; Student-Centered; Technology; Project-Based Learning; Instructor-Designed; Student-Driven

I. INTRODUCTION

While many schools in K-12 and higher education realize the importance of teaching foreign languages to prepare students to contribute to a better tomorrow, many obstacles present themselves limiting the teaching of foreign language in the United States and around the world. These obstacles include, but are not limited to, pedagogical, teacher-related, learner-related, and financial challenges, among many others [1].

The foreign language classroom, just like any other subject, has suffered from being teacher-centered and has struggled to find a balanced learning environment and to transition from being dominated by the teacher to being student-centered [2]. On page 88 of reference [3], the author cites Odom et al. stating that in today's classroom, students' attitude towards any subject is "positively associated with student-centered teaching practices and negatively associated with traditional (teacher-centered) teaching practices." Student-centeredness, however, requires, a shift-in-the-minds of both educators and students [4].

How do we promote this shift-in-the-thinking as educators? Available technological tools seem to make a difference in creating a healthy language learning environment that is also sustainable and affordable. The foreign language classroom is seeing more use of multimedia, moving toward student-centeredness, leaving behind the aging mentality of lecture-based instructions and teacher-dominated, teacher-centered classroom. This resolution to create a classroom atmosphere that puts the students in the center of their learning promotes a healthy relationship between the teacher and the learner, fosters critical thinking and shows the relevance of academic content to real life [5].

To highlight her efforts to overcome the roadblocks to a student-centered classroom, the author shares a success story of adopting a student-centered pedagogical approach to teaching Arabic. She encourages students to use existing tools to design their learning and think beyond the classroom walls by infusing technology into Project-Based Learning (PBL). In this paper, the author focuses on sharing her experience in implementing Technology Project-Based Learning in Introduction to Arabic I.

Elementary Arabic I is the beginner level course in Arabic language and culture. It is a course which covers and emphasizes the development of the basic skills of the Arabic language, including basic pronunciation, comprehension, communication, and grammar. Students in this course also become acquainted with the culture of the Arabic world [6]. This course may be offered in the traditional face-to-face, hybrid, synchronous, or asynchronous online environments. In a culminating, end-of-semester, instructor-designed assignment, students are required to create individual, digitally-recorded autobiographies. Clips of these autobiographies are to be included in a collaborative project, "Arabic 101 Class Documentary," in which the whole class contributes.

The following sections provide information on how Technology Project-Based Learning methodology is used to complete two teacher-designed projects in a beginning Arabic course. Additionally, future implications for the language and other classrooms are discussed:

- Section II offers background information on Project-Based Learning.
- Section III presents the design brief, including two hands-on, individual and whole class activities: "My Cultural Autobiography" and "Arabic 101 Class Documentary."
- Section IV shows how the two (individual and class semester projects) exemplify the characteristics of Technology Project-Based Learning (TPBL): using technology, taking

ownership, collaboration, and incorporating of the entire curriculum
- Section V introduces work samples of students' and a perspective on the benefit of TPBL in the Arabic classroom
- Section V is the conclusion. It contains a reflection and future implications for the language and other classes.

II. Background on Project-Based Learning

Project-based learning (PBL) is "an innovative approach to learning that teaches a multitude of strategies critical for success in the twenty-first century" [7]. It is known to help students take ownership of their learning and take pride in their accomplishments in an environment that invites creative thinking. Students practice collaboration, planning, problem-solving, communication, among other skills. They create projects, utilizing resources available to them, including technology, books, personal experiences, talents, and the Internet. Project-Based Learning incorporates the entire curriculum and encourages the exploration of multiple subjects while requiring a broad knowledge to complete tasks. John Savery defines PBL in reference [9] as "an instructional approach that has been used successfully for over 30 years and continues to gain acceptance in multiple disciplines".

III. The Design brief: Two Hands-on Learning Projects into One

Although they are due during the last week of class, the instructor shares "Arabic 101 Class Documentary," along with "My Cultural Autobiography," design brief several weeks before the conclusion of the course. At the time of introducing the two projects, students have learned the entire Arabic alphabet and can connect the letters to make words, spell (dictate) words, and pronounce words using correct grammar, special characters, and short and long vowels. Students have accumulated a substantial amount of vocabulary to cover different topics such as greetings, self-introduction, jobs, places of residence, family members, other people in their lives, and their likes and dislikes. They have learned to construct simple sentences, have taken several quizzes, and have completed a midterm exam. Students are encouraged to begin working on their individual and class projects early in the semester since they must finish their autobiographies in time to have their work included in the whole class documentary.

A. *"My Cultural Autobiography"- An Individual Project*

For this project, each student in Elementary Arabic I is expected to write and record his/her autobiography in Modern Standard Arabic. Students are expected to include the following information in their projects:

- A proper greeting
- Name and place(s) of residency
- Their field(s) of study
- The number of brothers and sisters they have, if any
- Favorites (Pets, food, colors, movies, drinks, etc.)
- Names of and information about other people in their lives (siblings, teachers, doctors, neighbors, etc.)

Each student is required to submit his/her English and Arabic versions of the written autobiography. They also create video recordings of the individual autobiography and upload them to the class online learning management system to present them to class. Students are graded as follows for this individual project:

- Five points for the submission of the Autobiography in English
- Five points for the Autobiography in Arabic
- Ten points for correct grammar
- Twenty points for correct pronunciation of individual words in Arabic and clarity of student's recorded voice
- Twenty points for using new vocabulary from each unit (7 words minimum)
- Ten points for helping at least one classmate peer-review his/her autobiography. Assessment of this task is accomplished through each student completing and submitting a form called "My Cultural Autobiography Evaluation Form."

B. *"Arabic 101 Class Documentary" – The Whole Class Project*

For 30 additional points, students collaborate to create a whole class documentary. In one video presentation, each student is asked to state her/his name, major of study, origin, citizenship, current home location, and the reason they are taking Arabic. The students' clips are edited and used as part of the final collaborative project. Each student is also required to complete an "Arabic 101 Class Documentary Survey" to share feedback with the instructor regarding difficulties experienced, students who were helpful or not, and their contributions in completing the class project.

IV. The Arabic Semester Projects - An Application of Technology Project-Based Learning

How does such a design brief in the Arabic classroom represent Technology Project-Based Learning? The above-presented design brief requires the use of technology while encouraging students to take ownership of their learning and work in collaboration with others.

A. *Using Technology*

To complete both their individual projects and the whole class documentary, students use technology across many stages of their work while communicating, collaborating, and presenting their products. They learn to use digital presentations, video production software and applications, and online collaboration and communication tools. They employ project planning, project management, production, and design tools such as video editing, storyboarding, and clip sequencing.

B. Taking Ownership

Another Technology Project-Based Learning (TPBL) is satisfied while implementing the mentioned summative assessment activity. To complete their work, students must take ownership of their learning. They carefully plan, manage, design, and execute the steps to present their stories. They express pride in their work, apply what they learned to their lives, and use their creations in real-life situations.

C. Collaboration

As a part of the requirements, students are asked to collaborate with classmates while working on their individual and whole class projects design. They use an evaluation form and a survey to self-evaluate their work and their classmates' contribution to the whole-class project. They evaluate how they and other classmates:

- Help one another in peer review
- Work together to accomplish project planning, project management, and task completion
- Work together to design the whole class video presentation

Another characteristic of Technology Project-Based Learning, i.e., collaboration, is satisfied by the requirement of cooperation and group-based learning among students. Everyone in the class uses his/her talent(s) to complete the final culminating project.

D. Incorporation of the Entire Curriculum

Designing activities that incorporate other academic subjects that focus on the whole student make learning an enjoyable experience and applicable to real life. Completing their individual autobiographies and the class documentary, students enjoy cross-disciplinary exploration. Students:

- Practice self-study and reflection
- Conduct writing critiques
- Explore the geography and climate of unfamiliar areas
- Recognize the names of other professions and fields of study in Arabic
- Learn about hobbies outside of their areas of interest
- Become familiar with diverse family structures and relationship styles
- Use multimedia and digital tools to design digital environments
- Participate in problem-solving, project planning, management, and communication

This design brief proves to incorporate many content areas such as critical thinking and writing, geography, social studies, family structure, multimedia, and project planning, management and communication.

V. REFLECTION AND STUDENTS WORK EXAMPLES

Following are two students' work samples of the Arabic autobiographies: Figure 1 and Figure 2. All identifying students' information (names, names of family members, school, origin, etc.) are removed from both work examples. In addition to the Arabic text, students also submit an English version of the autobiography to clarify any possible ambiguity in the Arabic language, if needed. The students also create a digital form of the autobiography that shows their pronunciation and fluency skills in Arabic.

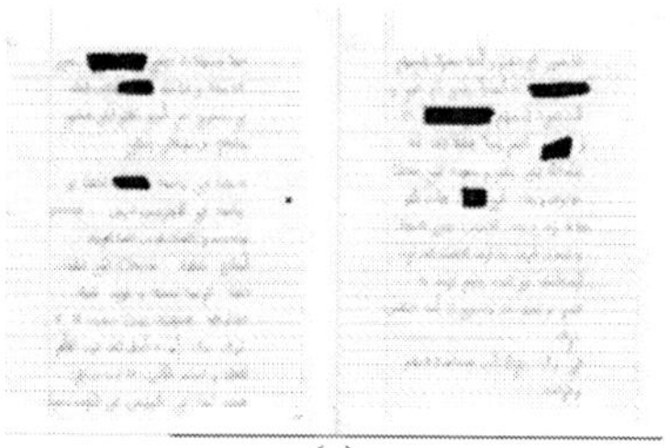

(a)

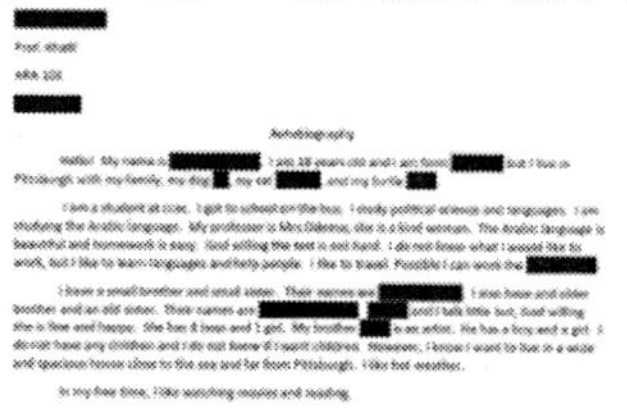

(b)

Figure 1. A Sample Female Student Written Autobiography in Elementary Arabic I: (a) Arabic Version and (b) English Version

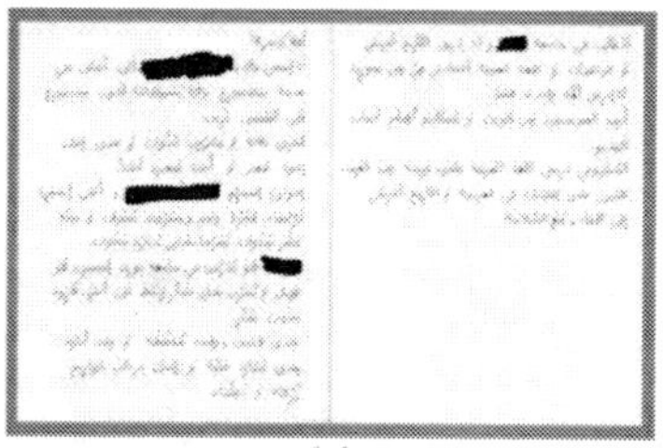

(a)

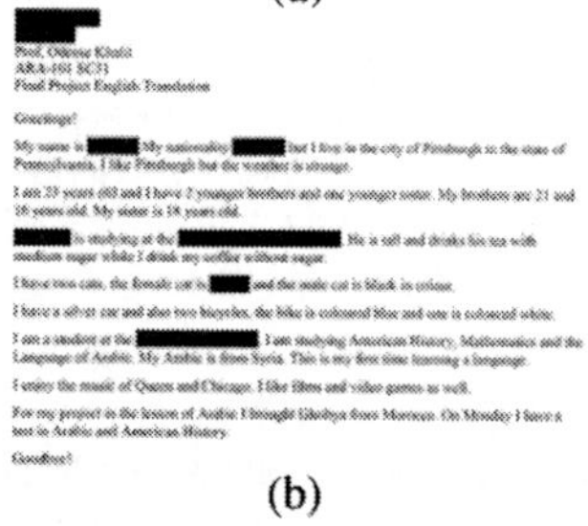

(b)

Figure 2. A Sample Male Student Written Autobiography in Elementary Arabic I: (a) Arabic Version and (b) English Version

Students in the above two examples share much about their lives, goals, and social circles. The information they provide includes a proper greeting to classmates, self and family introductions, hobbies, likes, and dislikes. It is remarkable to see how they put the language to use.

Wu [8] states that "Students write meaningful papers when they are allowed to explore various connections in writing" and that "writer-centered" project resulted in a "student-centered" writing classroom environment. After receiving the instructions for the final projects, the students begin to make connections between the academic content to their daily lives. They draft their autobiographies earlier in the semester and ask questions to clarify any possible unclear use of the language as they progress in their work. They become active learners, take control of achieving the project goals, use new vocabulary in context, and incorporating new vocabulary to add to their stories about themselves. Students are only allowed a limited number of non-course related vocabulary; therefore, during the writing process, students use force themselves to express what they want using the vocabulary they learned in the course. This approach is helpful since "contextualized vocabulary learning is more effective than learning words in lists" [9]. Putting the language to use empowers the learner, makes acquiring new vocabulary less tedious, and relates the knowledge gained in the classroom to real life. Moreover, students show excitement about being able to use that they produced in this final design brief in real life, especially in an interview where the Arabic language is preferred foreign language, with which to be familiar.

VI. CONCLUSION

Project-Based Learning has been a popular instructional approach to designing instructions for decades. It is the Technology part that is becoming a must-incorporate in every classroom. Technology removes obstacles and roadblocks, shortens distances, and promotes communications among scholars and the education community. Technology, when used correctly, equalizes the education field, spreads opportunities beyond the classroom and institutions walls, and removes obstacles in the way of preparing today's student to become a leader of better tomorrow.

To represent Technology Project-Based Learning (TPBL), an activity must use technology in a learner-centered, collaborative, innovative, and interdisciplinary environment [10].

As teacher-facilitated, student-driven approaches to learning, the end-of-semester culminating activities in Elementary Arabic I demonstrate Technology Project-Based Learning (TPBL) characteristics. In the foreign language classroom, TPBL is one of many pedagogical solutions to moving away from the unsuccessful concept of the teacher-centered classroom. It opens full doors for active learning and designing working solutions to real-world problems, but it is not the only approach. Many technology-infused pedagogies and instructional methodologies are also worth considering if they focus on the whole student and give him/her the center of the classroom.

An approach such as TPBL can be applied in many academic subjects to help educators and students reach diverse course objectives. [11]. Educators must provide opportunities for students to design, build, and create with their knowledge and the classroom becomes a heaven for fun while learning.

In 1916, John Dewey said, "Give the pupils something to do, not something to learn; and the doing is of such a nature as to demand thinking; learning naturally results" [3]. Technology Project-Based Learning requires students to use technology and their content knowledge to create solutions to real-world challenges. It enriches the learning environment and complements academic instruction and curricular design. It prepares 21st-century students to be innovative problem solvers in an ever-changing, technological world.

REFERENCES

[1] T. Elyas, and W. H. Al Grigri, "Obstacles to Teaching English in Saudi Arabia Public Schools: Teachers' and Supervisors' Perceptions," International Journal of Language Teaching, vol. 2, Sept. 2014. pp. 74-89.

[2] B. S. P. Teoh and T. K. Neo, " Interactive Multimedia Learning: Students' Attitudes and Learning Impact in an Animation Course," TOJET: The Turkish Online Journal of Educational Technology, vol. 6, Oct. 2007, pp. 28-37.

[3] A. L. Odom and C. V. Bell, "Associations of Middle School Student Science Achievement and Attitudes About Science with Student-Reported Frequency of Teacher Lecture Demonstrations and Student-Centered Learning," International Journal Of Environmental And Science Education, vol. 10, 2015, pp. 87-97, doi:10.12973/ijese.2015.232a.

[4] J. F. Strayer, "How Learning in an Inverted Classroom Influences Cooperation, Innovation, and Task Orientation," Learning Environments Research, vol. 15, 2012, pp. 171-193, doi:10.1007/s10984-012-9108-4.

[5] J. McTighe and G. Wiggins, Understanding by Design Professional Development Workbook. Association for Supervision and Curriculum Development (ASCD), 1703 North Beauregard Street, Alexandria, VA 22311.

[6] ARA 101 - Elementary Arabic 1. (n.d.). Retrieved Feb. 2019, from https://catalog.ccac.edu

[7] S. Bell, "Project-Based Learning for the 21st Century: Skills for the Future," The Clearing House, vol. 83, 2010, pp. 39-43, doi:10.1080/00098650903505415.

[8] R. Wu, "ESL Students Writing Autobiographies: Are there Any Connections?" Proc. Annual Meeting of the Rhetoric Society of America, Louisville, KY, May 1994, Retrieved Feb. 2019 from https://files.eric.ed.gov/fulltext/ED373325.pdf

[9] B. Nielsen, "A Review of Research into Vocabulary Learning and Acquisition," 2003, Retrieved Feb. 2019 from https://www.kushiro-ct.ac.jp/library/kiyo/kiyo36/Brian.pdf

[10] J. Savery, "Overview of Problem-Based Learning: Definitions and Distinctions," The Interdisciplinary Journal of Problem-Based Learning, vol. 1. May 2006, pp. 8-20.

[11] E. De Graaf, and A. Kolmos, "Characteristics of Problem-Based Learning," International Journal of Engineering Education, 2003, pp. 657-662.

Analysing Textual Content of Educational Web-Pages for Discovering Features useful for Classification Purposes

Vladimir Estivill-Castro, Matteo Lombardi and Alessandro Marani

School of Information and Communication Technology
Nathan Campus, Brisbane, 4111, QLD, Australia
Email: v.estivill-castro@griffith.edu.au
matteo.lombardi@griffithuni.edu.au alessandro.marani@griffithuni.edu.au

***Abstract*—Studies in Information Retrieval and Technology Enhanced Learning have not been able yet to propose reliable support to students and teachers when seeking educational resources on the Web. The driving force of web-search has been to match the topic of a query with the topic of documents. This paper involves Natural Language Learning approaches for an in-depth analysis of the common traits among educational web-pages. We analyzed the textual content of resources coming from educational websites and a survey among instructors. We computed more than 100 attributes and tested their significance for classification against web-pages from non-educational sources. Our analysis selected a set of 53 attributes. The results of a classification task prove that our traits allow for highly accurate filtering of resources with educational purposes. Moreover, the reliability of the proposed methodology is statistically verified.**

***Keywords*–Learning Objects; Internet based systems; Navigational aspects for on-line learning; Recommender Systems.**

I. Introduction

The Internet is among the most popular places students and teachers explore educational resources to support their educational tasks [1]. However, search engines like Google and other web-based recommender systems still struggle in suggesting web-pages matching to a specific purpose of interest, for example, *education* [2]. Automatically identifying web-content suitable for education is one of the most challenging objectives because it requires extraordinary attention.

Studies in Information Retrieval (IR) and Technology Enhanced Learning (TEL) have proposed several solutions to support teaching and learning needs of instructors and pupils within an enclosed platform [3] [4]. However, those research efforts have not been able yet to recommend a reliable tool that can leverage the potentially infinite amount of pedagogical resources hosted on the Internet for helping users during their educational tasks. As a result, after receiving recommendations from existing search engines, students and teachers must spend additional time and effort to filter only web-resources useful for education. Personalization has improved web-search by identifying what topics users prefer, and some progress has been achieved in deducing the purpose of the search (e.g., the user is about to book a trip) for tailored advertising [5]; however, this is a very different use of recommendation. Instead, we focus here on identifying documents with a purpose in the sense of being of value for a learning objective.

Our exploration covers more than 2,300 web-pages obtained from the Seminarsonly website [6], and other sources human instructors [7] identified as relevant for teaching. We incorporate semantic technologies when processing natural language to we elicit more than 100 features computed directly from the text of web-resources. We analyze our features to discover which of these become attributes that permit a clear distinction between resources suitable for education and those not suitable. The resulting feature set is evaluated performing a binary classification of items in our dataset. We built such dataset labeling the aforementioned educational web-pages as "relevant for education". We labeled as "not relevant for education" pages crawled from the former DMOZ Web directory, currently known as Curlie [8]. Our evaluation covers learning with several representatives of classification algorithms. We apply Student's t-test to strengthen the validity of our feature set. In particular, we tested the accuracy distribution across the results of a 30-fold cross validation when using all the selected traits, and when reducing the feature space utilizing Principal Component Analysis (PCA) and Support Vector Machine (SVM). The t-test confirms that all the features are essential for achieving the best accuracy in our filtering task for each classifier.

Section II which describes our data-set. Section III describes or features. Our evaluation methods appears in Section IV. Section V reports experimental results. Section VI contrast our work and Section VII provides conclusions.

II. Data analysis

We involved Semantic Web techniques and organized the information into semantic entities extracted from the textual content of web-pages, where a *semantic entity* is an instance of a DBpedia [9] resource that groups a collection of properties. Semantic entities can be associated with one or more consecutive words. Following other contributions [10] [11] [12], we use the Dandelion API [13] for deducing all the semantic entities in text. In our case, we simplify the analysis of complex and articulated texts by considering the semantic entities extracted from them as their representation. We suggest that, when the text is an educational resource, semantic entities contain the most distinctive pieces of information about what the content, concepts, knowledge and skills educators deliver through the text. Hence, we expect that a set of entities will represent the entire text reflecting the same knowledge content without losing any proper traits.

A. The dataset

Our goal is to extract features from web-pages and test their validity to recognize whether or not a web-page is suitable for educational purposes. Hence, the items in our dataset are web-pages with two possible values for the class: TRUE, when a resource has been declared relevant for teaching some concepts, or FALSE when the page does not contain educational content. Our dataset consists of more than 2,300 educational web-pages we extracted from two different sources. The first source is the Seminarsonly website, which hosts content about Computer Science, Mechanical, Civic and Electrical Engineering, as well as Chemical and Biomedical sciences among others. The second source of educational material is a subset of web-pages ranked by instructors during a survey [7]. The survey's first phase automatically used queries by an intelligent system against a search engine with names of educational concepts and courses. The second phase exposed groups of 10 retrieved pages to instructors who judged the suitability of the web-page as a learning-object suitable for teaching. In particular, whether the page could support the learning of the concepts of the query in the originator course. The instructors used a 5-point Likert scale to rank how likely would they use that web-page for teaching a concept. When web-pages are highly ranked uniformly by judges, it is certain that the page is suitable for being used in an educational context. For that reason, in this analysis, a web-page is labelled as TRUE ("relevant for education") only when it collected 3 points (relevant) or more (where the maximum is 5 points —- Strongly relevant) in the survey. Other pages from the survey are discarded. On the other hand, we obtain the web-pages classified as FALSE ("non-relevant for teaching") by the crawling of URLs contained into the DMOZ open directory. In particular, we included pages coming from all the 15 categories represented in DMOZ, resulting in more than 3,200 web-pages. We consider those web-resources not suitable for teaching. In total, our dataset consists of around 5,600 labelled web-pages, according to their usability in educational contexts.

B. Extraction of Semantic Entities

We exploit DBpedia entities extracted from web-pages for deducing information about the content of a whole page. For each extracted entity, Dandelion also reports a confidence value for that association. The higher the confidence, the more reliable the link between the part of the text and the entity. The tool also allows to select a threshold of minimum confidence for the extraction, avoiding to retrieve poorly related entities. Hence, the higher the confidence threshold, the higher the effectiveness of the extraction process but, on the other hand, the number of entities extracted tends to decrease when the threshold is high. DBpedia also offers the *type* of an entity: places, companies and personal names. When no match is found, Dandelion assigns the type *Concept* to the entity (refer to Figure 1).

III. Feature Elicitation Process

We analyze four parts of each web-page separately: the *Title*, the *Body*, the *Links* and the *Highlights*. We extract the last two from the body itself of the page. In particular, the *Title* is extracted from the title tag and the *Body* element from the body tag. Then, inside the *Body* tag, the text between the anchor $< a >$ tags is concatenated and labeled as the *Links*, while we obtain the *Highlights* by merging the text between the tags $< h1 >$, $< h2 >$, $< h3 >$, $< b >$ and $< strong >$. In this way, we separate all the four elements of a web-page, allowing for a thorough analysis of the page itself.

We apply the same approach to all the four parts of a web-page. In the end, we may find a feature that is significant for classification purposes when considering a specific part of the page (e.g., the *Links*), while the same feature could be discarded for a different part (for instance, the *Title*). For that reason, we run the Dandelion API Entity Extraction tool on all the resources in our dataset, considering one part of a web-page at a time, so that the entities will also have a label that indicates the part of a page from which they originated.

The following sections present the groups of features extracted from our resources. For each group, we selected the semantic entities according to four different thresholds for the confidence: the default 0.6, then 0.7, 0.8 and finally 0.9.

A. Lexical features

We base the first group of features on NLP for discovering characteristics and quantity of the terms used in a web-page. In particular, the following attributes exploit the complexity of the words, as well as the number of semantic entities and concepts relative to the length of a text.

1. The Complex_Words_Ratio $= \frac{\text{\# complex words}}{\text{\# words}}$ is is the ratio of the number of complex words on the total number of words (i.e., the length) in a text. We used the Fathom API [14] for deducing the quantity of complex words: words composed by three or more syllables.
2. Feature Number_entities is the total # of entities of any type extracted from a text.
3. Entities_By_Words $= \frac{\text{\# entities}}{\text{\# words}}$ is the number of entities extracted from a text, with respect to the total number of words. This feature measures how many words it is necessary to read for finding a semantic entity.
4. Concepts_By_Words $= \frac{\text{\# concept entities}}{\text{\# words}}$ is a feature similar to the Entities_By_Words, but considering only the concept-type entities. The idea is to have an insight into how many words it is necessary to read for finding a concept.
5. Concepts_By_Entities $= \frac{\text{\# concepts}}{\text{\# entities}}$ reports the fraction of entities that are also concepts, with respect to the total number of entities found in a text.

B. Features based on Semantic Density

Researchers in TEL refer to *Semantic Density* (SD) as the quantity of topics presented by a resource with respect to a characteristic of the resource itself. For instance, the IEEE Learning Object Metadata schema defines the Semantic Density of a resource as the ratio of the number of concepts taught on the length of the resource (commonly measured in minutes or hours). As a result, a resource yields high SD when many topics are squeezed in a short time frame.

We consider the different entities in a text as topics delivered by a resource. Then, we measure two different SD values for a text: one value concerning the number of words, and the other related to the reading time (similarly to the aforementioned IEEE standard). For an even more comprehensive analysis of the text, we also take into account only the concept entities. In the end, we compute SD of a web-page using four attributes.

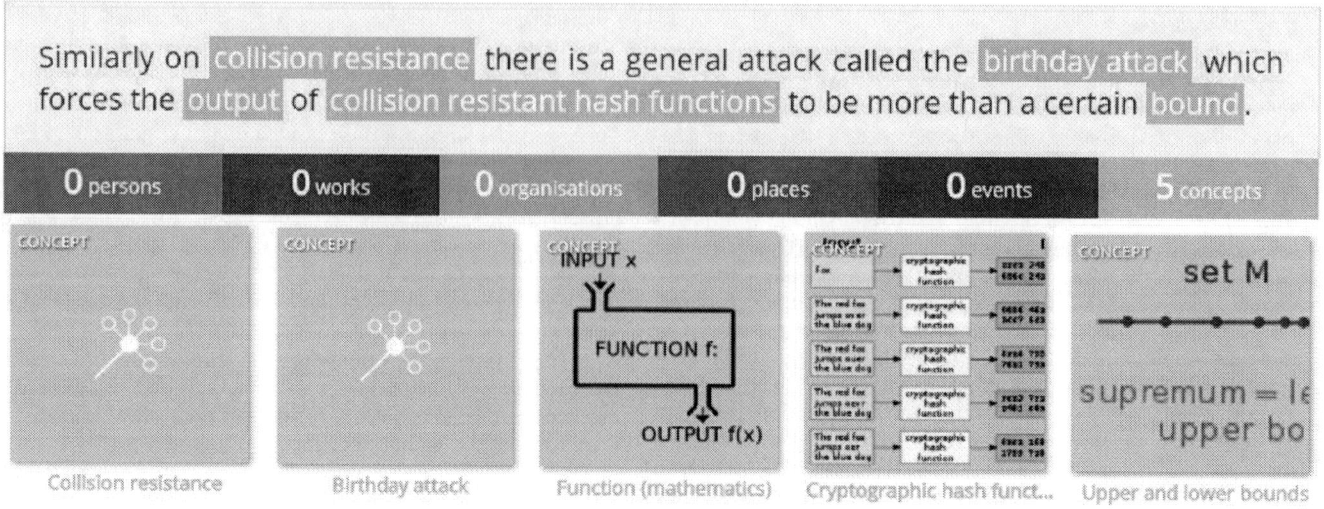

Figure 1. Entities in a text found by Dandelion API.

1. $\text{SD\_By\_Words} = \frac{|\text{Entities}|}{\#\ \text{words}}$ measures how many distinct entities Dandelion extracted from the text (i.e., the set of discussed topics), with respect to the number of words. When two texts have similar quantities of words, the one with more distinct entities is the denser.
2. Similarly to the previous feature, $\text{SD\_By\_ReadingTime} = \frac{|\text{Entities}|}{\text{reading time}}$ is now measured in relation to the reading time of the text. In this case, the text is denser when the reading time is low, and the number of distinct entities (i.e., topics) is high.
3. $\text{SD\_Concepts\_By\_Words} = \frac{|\text{Concepts}|}{\#\ \text{words}}$ considers only distinct concept entities, with respect to the number of words. In educational texts, concept-type entities are more frequent than other types. Hence, the concept-based SD is expected to hold significant information for educational classification.
4. $\text{SD\_Concepts\_By\_ReadingTime} = \frac{|\text{Concepts}|}{\text{reading time}}$ measures the quantity of concepts taught by a text according to the expected reading time. As an example, let us consider two texts where Dandelion extracted the same amount of distinct concepts. In that case, the text which requires less reading time presents concepts in a more condensed way, so it holds higher SD than its counterpart. In essence, less time is spent for other entities (i.e., non-concepts) that are not likely to be used in educational resources, while important concepts receive more attention.

C. Selection of the most promising features

At this stage, nine groups of numerical features represent each web-page. In our dataset, the content of a single item is split across four web-elements. Furthermore, for each element of a page, entities are extracted at four different thresholds, except for the Complex_Words_Ratio group, which leverages only natural language text so it does not require semantic entities extraction. Since the first four attributes in the count are those that involve the ratio of complex words, and we include one feature for each element of the page, we have

$$\#\ \text{potential\_features} = 4 + 8 * 4 * 4 = 132\ \text{features}.$$

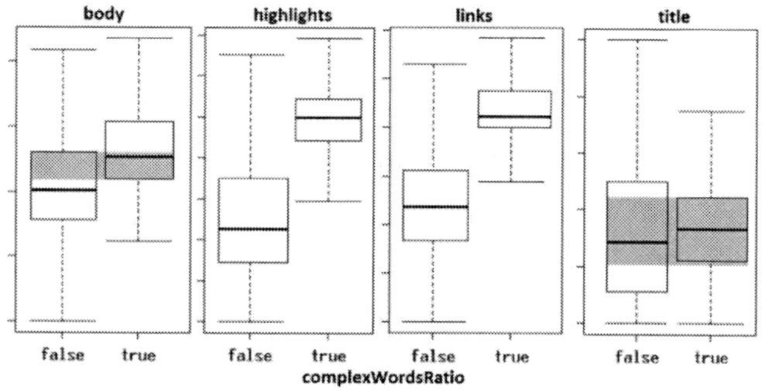

Figure 2. The distribution of the four features in the Complex_Words_Ratio group, according to the class.

However, some of those features may not be useful to discriminate between a resource relevant for education and one not suitable for that purpose. We use a parallel coordinate visualization [15] of groups of features and we select only the traits where a visual distinction is clear among the web-pages in our dataset. Our filtering process is performed according to the distribution of the values of each feature, and we now explain it in the following paragraphs. The criterion for selecting or discarding a feature is that there is no overlap between the most frequent values of the TRUE and FALSE distributions, namely, the values from the first quartile (Q1) to the third quartile (Q3) in a box plot representation. In the interest of saving space, we discuss only the first two groups of features and show the box plots for their distributions. The first group is **Complex_Words_Ratio**. Figure 2 illustrates that the *Highlights* and the *Links* distributions overlap between classes only across the quartiles Q1 and Q3. The area in gray highlights that most of the values from first to third quartile are in common for the *Body* and *Title* elements, while *Highlights* and *Links* are able to separate TRUE and FALSE items with high accuracy. But the *Body* and *Title* distributions display significant commonality for the their most frequent values. Hence, the two features

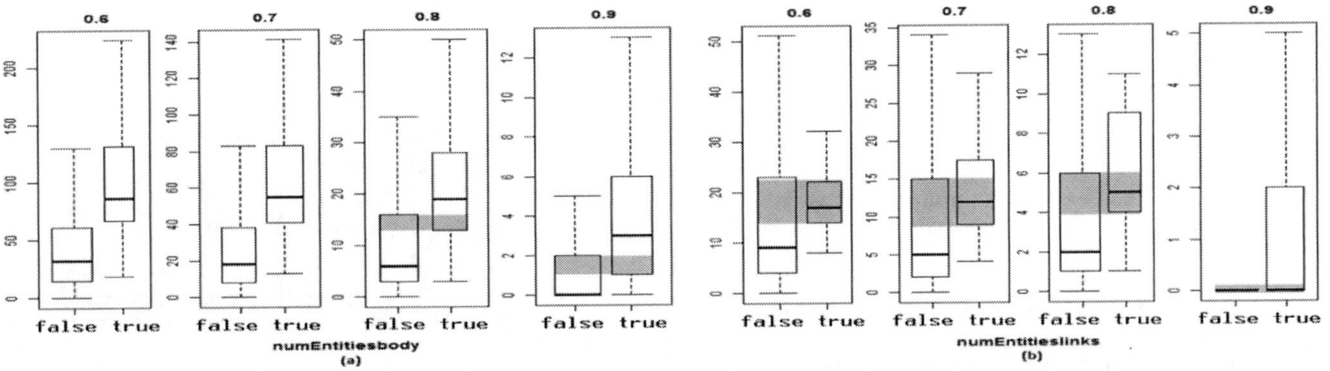

Figure 3. Analysis of TRUE and FALSE items distributions for features in the **Number_entities** group, extracted from *Body* (a) and *Links* (b) elements of a web-page. The gray areas indicate an overlap.

TABLE I. THE 53 ATTRIBUTES SELECTED FOR THE OVERALL FEATURE SET, DENOTED BY A ⋆ SYMBOL.

Group	*Body* .6	.7	.8	*Links* .6	.7	.8	*Highlights* .6	.7	.8	*Title* .6	.7	.8
Complex_Words_Ratio					⋆			⋆				
Number_entities	⋆	⋆								⋆	⋆	
Entities_By_Words	⋆	⋆		⋆	⋆	⋆						
Concepts_By_Words	⋆	⋆	⋆	⋆	⋆	⋆	⋆	⋆				
Concepts_By_Entities	⋆	⋆	⋆	⋆	⋆	⋆						
SD_By_Words				⋆	⋆	⋆	⋆	⋆	⋆			
SD_By_ReadingTime				⋆	⋆	⋆	⋆	⋆	⋆			
SD_Concepts _By_Words	⋆	⋆	⋆	⋆	⋆	⋆	⋆	⋆				
SD_Concepts _By_ReadingTime	⋆	⋆	⋆	⋆	⋆	⋆	⋆	⋆				

selected for this group are Complex_Words_Ratio_*Links* and Complex_Words_Ratio_*Highlights*, while the others are discarded. Moving to the **Number_entities** group, there are 16 possible combinations amongst 4 threshold values and 4 elements of the web-page. Here we show 8 of those potential attributes. The first four from the left (Figure 3a) are about the count of entities found in the *Body* considering the four values of confidence thresholds, while the others (Figure 3b) consider just entities found among the *Links*. Only 2 out of 8 attributes are useful for classification. They are Number_entities_*Body*_0.6 and Number_entities_*Body*_0.7, because all the other distributions overlap between TRUE and FALSE items. Interestingly, when threshold is 0.9, the number of entities dramatically decreases in both educational and non-educational web-pages. Especially among the latter group, there are only form 0 to 2 entities in the *Body*, and none in the *Links*. Since all the features computed at threshold 0.9 experience the same decrease, in order to have a fair comparison, we discard them. The remaining 8 traits for this group are computed taking into account the *Highlights* and *Title* elements. In the first case, all the distributions overlap so none of the attributes is selected. About *Title*, distributions of entities at threshold 0.6 and 0.7 do not overlap so they are selected, while raising the threshold to 0.8 the two distributions overlap. We apply the same methodology to the other groups. What features are selected as discriminators by the above analysis is summarized in Table I. Note that group Complex_Words_Ratio does not require entity extraction, therefore, it has only one attribute per page element.

IV. METHODOLOGY FOR EVALUATION

In the evaluation phase, we aim to see whether or not the 53 proposed attributes allow state-of-the-art classifiers to achieve high accuracy in recognizing the web-pages labeled as relevant for education in our dataset. In order to achieve that goal, we applied popular feature selection algorithms to our set of traits, and then we compared the accuracy on the same set of classifiers. The rationale behind our choice is that some features may be discarded by generic algorithms as not useful or redundant, or combined to obtain a new set of attributes. However, in case the overall accuracy decreases applying feature selection methods, we can conclude that the proposed features allow classifiers to yield higher performance in an educational task, thus, all 53 traits are important when filtering web-pages in such field. The algorithms for feature selection chosen as baselines in this work are Principal Component Analysis - PCA [16] and Support Vector Machine - SVM [17].

A. Classifiers and evaluation measure

In order to produce a comprehensive evaluation across all types of machine-learning algorithms for classification, we used state-of-the-art classifiers belonging to four families, namely Bayesian, Rule-based, Function-based, and Tree-based classifiers, for a total of eight algorithms. From the first family, we chose **Bayesian Network** built with hill-climbing method [18]. The three rule-based methods involved are **Decision Table** [19], **Repeated Incremental Pruning to Produce Error Reduction - RIPPER** [20] and **Partial decision list - PART** [21]. From the function-based classifiers we selected **Logistic** [22] and **Sequential Minimal Optimization - SMO** [23]. Finally, as tree-based classifiers, we opted for **J48**, which builds a pruned C4.5 decision tree [24], and the popular **RandomForest** algorithm [25]. We used the default implementation and parameters provided by WEKA for all classification methods. We recorded the performance of the classifiers on a 30-fold Cross Validation according to their **Average Precision (AP)**, which is the mean of the **Precision (P)** in a classification task across all the 30 folds:

$$P(f) = \frac{\text{\# correctly classified items}}{\text{\# items}} \quad , \quad AP = \sum_{f \in folds} \frac{P(f)}{\text{\# folds}}.$$

where f is the i-th fold, and # folds is 30 in this study. We present our results in the next section as percentage values.

In addition, we aim to strengthen our claim performing a statistical analysis of our feature set against those generated by PCA and SVM, comparing the distribution of P in all the folds using the Student's paired T-test. The null hypothesis h_0 to be investigated is:

$$h_0 = \text{The chosen feature set does not influence P.}$$

While the alternative hypothesis h_1 is:

$$h_1 = \text{P is higher when using all 53 features.}$$

If h_0 is significantly rejected and h_1 confirmed, we demonstrate the actual validity of all the attributes proposed in this work. To verify at least a 95% of such significance, we look for values of $p<0.05$ in our T-tests. We ran PCA, SVM and the classifiers using the WEKA 8.3.2 Java library with default parameters. The entire evaluation is performed on a Windows 10 machine, with Intel i7-6700 octa-core processor @ 3.4GHz and 32GB of RAM.

V. RESULTS

As described in Section IV, we applied two state-of-the-art feature selection algorithms, PCA and SVM, to build two sets of attributes we will use as baselines throughout our evaluation. To achieve a more comprehensive comparison, we created those two sets differently. The first one, called *PCA*, is obtained running PCA on our dataset. The number of resulting components, in this case, is fourteen. The second set of traits comes from SVM, a method for ranking features. We selected the ten most valuable attributes according to the SVM algorithm, forming the *Top10-SVM* feature set.

Figure 4 shows the AP measured when running different classifiers using the two aforementioned baselines, and our 53 attributes. We call our feature set *AllFeatures*. In every test performed, the proposed set *AllFeatures* allows classifiers to obtain the highest precision in average on the 30 folds of the cross-validation testing. However, we also performed statistical testing to verify if we can reject the null hypothesis h_0 (namely, "there is no evidence that the chosen feature set influences the precision of a classifier") and accept the alternative h_1. In particular, since we have two baselines, two alternative hypotheses will be verified:
h_1^{PCA} = *"A classifier achieves higher precision when considering all features than the ones by PCA"*
h_1^{SVM} = *"A classifier achieves higher precision when considering all features than the ones by SVM"*.

Table II reports the results of the Student's T-test performed in our evaluation. We verified a significance of at least 95% for our hypotheses considering each classifier. We reached higher statistical significance, around 99% (p-value<0.01) for h_1^{PCA} on the majority of the classifiers. Only **BayesNet** has a slightly higher p-value (0.01359). However, it is still lower than 0.05. When testing our 53 features against those labeled most important by SVM, also h_1^{SVM} is accepted with 99% or more significance on all the algorithms but one. Indeed, the p-value when using **DecisionTable** is 0.01688, yet smaller than the required threshold of 0.05.

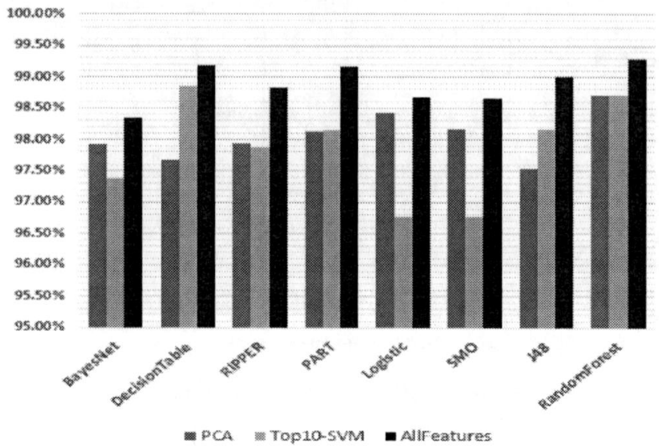

Figure 4. The average precision (AP) computed for each classifier when using the different feature sets analyzed in our evaluation process.

TABLE II. STUDENT'S T-TEST RESULTS FOR EACH CLASSIFIER. THE DESIRED p-VALUE <0.05 IS INDICATED WITH "*", A p-VALUE <0.01 IS LABELED WITH "**".

Classifier	*AllFeatures* vs. *PCA*		*AllFeatures* vs. *Top10-SVM*	
	T	p-value	T	p-value
BayesNet	2.3266	0.01359 *	7.3054	2.39E-08 **
DecisionTable	6.5606	1.73E-07 **	2.2284	0.01688 *
RIPPER	5.0055	1.25E-05 **	4.8125	2.14E-05 **
PART	5.2519	6.30E-06 **	5.2318	6.66E-06 **
Logistic	2.5343	0.008463 **	10.15	2.35E-11 **
SMO	4.0649	0.0001677 **	9.6948	6.64E-11 **
J48	7.6944	8.73E-09 **	4.4585	5.69E-05 **
RandomForest	4.2105	0.0001126 **	4.3679	7.31E-05 **

VI. RELATED WORK

Extraction and selection of attributes from a text is a popular research topic [26] [27]. Recently proposed approaches are also based on alternative methods from other research fields. For instance, [28] applied a technique for encoding signals called Wavelet Packet Transform for web-page analysis. Also deep learning methods like Convolutional Recurrent Neural Network [29] have been applied for the classification of relations in texts. To elicit features useful for filtering educational web-resources, our approach leverages techniques for analysing texts coming from the Knowledge Management, Information Retrieval and the Semantic Web communities. In the field of Education, [12] used semantic entities from DBpedia to describe and enrich texts coming from the Coursera [30]. platform.

Additional criteria have been suggested when dealing with content from the Web: Several studies shown how latent information can be found analysing both text and structure of web-pages. [31] suggested a methodology for deducing the category of a web-page considering the loading time of different objects like images, CSS theme, Javascript code and Flash content. However, only a group of 6 categories can be deducted, and educational-related ones are not part of it. Also, [32] proposed a more general approach which takes into account the fields of web-pages such as title, body and anchor text (i.e., the text used to embody a URL) for evaluating datasets of web-pages. [33] demonstrated that links in a web-page are important for automatic classification; thus these authors exploited links for deducing pages of academic institutions. However, their work is about identifying pages useful for extracting the internal organization of an Institute, rather than educational resources delivered in educational coursework.

VII. CONCLUSIONS

We examined a dataset of more than 5,600 web-pages with the goal of identifying the purpose of a web-page (suitability as an educational resource). This is a very different task than recognizing the subject matter nor the topic of a web-page. We attack this problem by seeking what features can be extracted from web-pages and their content. We proposed and identified those useful for classifying online resources for the purpose of education. We incorporated techniques from both natural language processing and semantic analysis for the definition of an initial set of 132 potential predictors. Then, the most promising traits are the output of an in-depth feature selection process which results in a set of 53 characteristics extracted from four sections of a web-page (see Table I). We evaluated the validity of our proposed features on the binary classification task that discriminates whether the purpose of the web-page is educational. In particular, we performed a 30-fold cross-validation test on our dataset using several state-of-the-art classifiers of many types and learning models. As baselines, we used feature selection algorithms for reducing the number of attributes according to two general approaches: PCA and SVM. We demonstrated that the average precision (AP) across the folds is higher when using our suggested 53 features. Furthermore, results of Student's T-test strengthen our proposal with all test repetitions achieving p-value < 0.05, and many lower than 0.01. This statistical significance at very high levels for all classifiers confirms the features are informative and effective in providing discrimination capacity to classifiers across several families. We expect our work to facilitate retrieval and recommendation of web resources suitable for specific purposes, especially for helping students and teachers in educational tasks.

REFERENCES

[1] H. Drachsler, K. Verbert, O. C. Santos, and N. Manouselis, "Panorama of recommender systems to support learning," in Recommender systems handbook. Springer, 2015, pp. 421–451.

[2] M. Lombardi and A. Marani, "A comparative framework to evaluate recommender systems in technology enhanced learning: a case study," in Advances in Artificial Intelligence and Its Applications. Springer, 2015, pp. 155–170.

[3] C. Limongelli, M. Lombardi, A. Marani, F. Sciarrone, and M. Temperini, "A recommendation module to help teachers build courses through the moodle learning management system," New Review of Hypermedia and Multimedia, vol. 22, no. 1–2, 2015, pp. 58–82.

[4] S. Sergis and D. Sampson, "Learning object recommendations for teachers based on elicited ict competence profiles," Learning Technologies, IEEE Transactions on, 2015, pp. 67–80.

[5] J. Arora, S. Agrawal, P. Goyal, and S. Pathak, "Extracting entities of interest from comparative product reviews," in Conf. on Information and Knowledge Management. ACM, 2017, pp. 1975–1978.

[6] Seminarsonly, http://www.seminarsonly.com/.

[7] A. Marani, "WebEduRank: an educational ranking principle of web pages for teaching," Ph.D. dissertation, Griffith University, 2018.

[8] Curlie, https://curlie.org/.

[9] DBpedia, http://wiki.dbpedia.org/.

[10] D. Taibi, R. Rogers, I. Marenzi, W. Nejdl, Q. A. I. Ahmad, and G. Fulantelli, "Search as research practices on the web: The sar-web platform for cross-language engine results analysis," in 8th ACM Conf. on Web Science, ser. WebSci '16. New York, NY, USA: ACM, 2016, pp. 367–369.

[11] M. Brambilla, S. Ceri, E. Della Valle, R. Volonterio, and F. X. Acero Salazar, "Extracting emerging knowledge from social media," in 26th Int. Conf. on World Wide Web, 2017, pp. 795–804.

[12] C. Limongelli, M. Lombardi, A. Marani, and D. Taibi, "Enrichment of the dataset of joint educational entities with the web of data," in Advanced Learning Technologies (ICALT), IEEE 17th Int. Conf. on. IEEE, 2017, pp. 528–529.

[13] Dandelion, https://dandelion.eu/.

[14] Fathom, search.cpan.org/dist/Lingua-EN-Fathom/lib/Lingua/EN/Fathom.pm.

[15] A. Inselberg, Parallel Coordinates: Visual Multidimensional Geometry and Its Applications. Berlin, Heidelberg: Springer-Verlag, 2009.

[16] S. Wold, K. Esbensen, and P. Geladi, "Principal component analysis," Chemometrics and intelligent laboratory systems, vol. 2, no. 1-3, 1987, pp. 37–52.

[17] I. Guyon, J. Weston, S. Barnhill, and V. Vapnik, "Gene selection for cancer classification using support vector machines," Machine learning, vol. 46, no. 1, 2002, pp. 389–422.

[18] G. F. Cooper and E. Herskovits, "A bayesian method for the induction of probabilistic networks from data," Machine learning, vol. 9, no. 4, 1992, pp. 309–347.

[19] R. Kohavi, "The power of decision tables," in 8th European Conf. on Machine Learning, ser. ECML'95. Springer, 1995, pp. 174–189.

[20] W. W. Cohen, "Fast effective rule induction," in 12th Int. Conf. on Machine Learning, A. Prieditis and S. J. Russell, Eds. Morgan Kaufmann, July 9th-12th 1995, pp. 115–123.

[21] E. Frank and I. H. Witten, "Generating accurate rule sets without global optimization," in 15ht Int. Conf. on Machine Learning, ser. ICML '98. San Francisco, CA, USA: Morgan Kaufmann, 1998, pp. 144–151.

[22] S. Le Cessie and J. C. Van Houwelingen, "Ridge estimators in logistic regression," Applied statistics, 1992, pp. 191–201.

[23] J. C. Platt, "Fast training of support vector machines using sequential minimal optimization," in Advances in Kernel Methods - Support Vector Learning, B. Schölkopf, C. J. C. Burges, and A. J. Smola, Eds. Cambridge, MA, USA: MIT Press, January 1998, pp. 185–208.

[24] J. R. Quinlan, "C 4.5: Programs for machine learning," The Morgan Kaufmann Series in Machine Learning, San Mateo, CA, 1993.

[25] L. Breiman, "Random forests," Machine learning, vol. 45, no. 1, 2001, pp. 5–32.

[26] Y. Yang and J. O. Pedersen, "A comparative study on feature selection in text categorization," in ICML, vol. 97, 1997, pp. 412–420.

[27] M. J. Paul, "Feature selection as causal inference: Experiments with text classification," in 21st Conf. on Computational Natural Language Learning (CoNLL), 2017, pp. 163–172.

[28] A. Mahajan, S. Roy, and S. Jat, "Feature selection for short text classification using wavelet packet transform," in 19th Conf. on Computational Natural Language Learning, 2015, pp. 321–326.

[29] D. Raj, S. Sahu, and A. Anand, "Learning local and global contexts using a convolutional recurrent network model for relation classification in biomedical text," in 21st Conf. on Computational Natural Language Learning (CoNLL), 2017, pp. 311–321.

[30] Coursera, https://www.coursera.org/.

[31] M. Butkiewicz, H. V. Madhyastha, and V. Sekar, "Characterizing web page complexity and its impact," IEEE/ACM Trans. on Networking, vol. 22, no. 3, 2014, pp. 943–956.

[32] S. Robertson, H. Zaragoza, and M. Taylor, "Simple bm25 extension to multiple weighted fields," in 13th ACM Int. Conf. on Information and knowledge management. ACM, 2004, pp. 42–49.

[33] P. Kenekayoro, K. Buckley, and M. Thelwall, "Automatic classification of academic web page types," Scientometrics, vol. 101, no. 2, 2014, pp. 1015–1026.

Software System for Automatic Creation of Operation Manuals for Real-Time Use by Students During Lectures

Naoki Morita
Graduate School of Information and Telecommunication Engineering
Tokai University
Tokyo, Japan
e-mail: morita@tokai.ac.jp

Kenta Morita
Graduate School of Engineering
Mie University
Mie, Japan
e-mail: k-morita@ip.elec.mie-u.ac.jp

Abstract – **Recently, classes in which students use their own Personal Computers (PCs) to follow lecture instructions are becoming increasingly commonplace. However, in situations where students are unable to fully understand a portion of an ongoing lecture or have missed portions of the instructor's explanation due to late arrival, it is unlikely that they will be able to catch up with and track ongoing explanations and/or perform operations in tandem with the instructor. However, it is also burdensome for the instructors that have prepared such classroom materials to alter their lessons to accommodate students who are late or having difficulties. Accordingly, we developed a system that automatically creates operation manuals for real-time use by students during lectures and confirmed that students who were late for classes in which it was used could recover from such delays on their own.**

Keywords - Operation manual; Automatic creation; Computer-assisted instructions; Global hook

I. MOTIVATION

Recently, classes in which students use their own Personal Computers (PCs) to learn how to use applications, such as Microsoft Word or Excel, or to practice programming techniques, have become increasingly commonplace. In such classes, the instructor projects their desktop display onto a screen that is used to demonstrate how the software is used and to show students how to perform operations.

Normally, the screen changes that result from the instructor's actions are explained just before a new window appears, and the instructor typically clarifies what s/he intends to do by highlighting the operation target with the mouse cursor. However, not all students are always able to hear and understand the instructor's explanations and students who lose track of an operation in progress will be unable to perform that operation independently.

In an earlier study, Bandoh et al. developed a system that uses two screens, one displaying the state before an operation and the other displaying the expected result [1]. This system allows students to recognize the before and after conditions for an operation at a glance. However, the problem with this system is that explanations regarding the corresponding operation are limited, and the system only displays the most current operations. Hence, students whose understanding of the operations is incomplete will be unable to follow the entire demonstration. Additionally, students will be unable to review the operation after the lecture.

In another study, Itamiya et al. developed a lecture recording system that can superimpose blackboard-writing and images from the lecturer's PC screen on the student's device in real time using a video camera [2]. However, since the required operations are performed during the lesson while explanations are provided, long intervals tend to occur between operations and the efforts required to confirm student comprehension levels may be inappropriate during lectures.

Furthermore, students who are late to attending the instructor's demonstration need the ability to rapidly configure their devices to the same state as the lecturer's PC, which means that they have to compensate for the lack instructions regarding the operations they missed. To address such issues, the creation of an instruction manual would be very desirable. The use of manual creation software [3][4], makes it possible for instructors to reduce the labor involved when creating lecture materials to a certain extent, but it remains very time consuming to create such detailed manuals.

In this paper, we discuss the process of creating lecture materials without requiring additional labor in Section II. Section III explains our newly developed system, and Section IV summarizes our work.

II. CONCEPT

The ultimate goal of our research is to enable all students to operate their PCs in tandem with their instructor's operations and provide a way for students who do not fully understand previous operations, or who have arrived at the lecture late, to compensate for their incomplete knowledge. However, as noted above, it is usually very time consuming for instructors to create such detailed manuals.

The purpose of this research is to provide a system that creates an operation manual of an ongoing lecture for student use without requiring any special work on the part of the lecturer. To accomplish this, it is necessary to provide a method by which they can quickly grasp the operation target and perform any required operations they have missed or do not understand. However, since this must be done while the lecture is in progress, students must first complete those missed operations and advance their screens to match the instructor's PC in the shortest period of time possible.

Our newly developed system creates a screenshot of the instructor's PC at each operation change, that students can watch as a slideshow. More specifically, first the system creates a screenshot of the instructor's PC window just before an operation. Second, based on the operation of the active window, it extracts the operation target. Third, the system highlights the targeted operation on the captured image and inserts a text explanation of how the operation is performed (such as via a left mouse click). Finally, the edited image capture is sent to a Web server.

Since each of these tasks is performed in real-time every time the instructor performs an operation, students who are late or unable to attend the lecture, or who need help understanding the processes involved, can review the entire process on the Web server.

III. Developed System

The system developed in this study consists of an operation log storage module on the instructor's PC and an operation log publish module on the Web server. In the subsections below, we will explain these modules, the results used in the class, and then discuss the system.

A. Storage Module

This module runs on the Windows 10 Operating System (OS). During operation, the instructor's application constantly exchanges messages with the OS regarding keyboard and mouse input operations. Our system monitors these messages using Global Hook technology and extracts all WM_LBUTTONDOWN messages (left mouse button clicks), WM_RBUTTONDOWN messages (right mouse button clicks), WM_KEYDOWN messages (press any key operations), and WM_MENUSELECT messages for the active window. As a result, all of the required information is extracted without the need for any special operations other than the instructor's demonstration.

Figures 1(a) to 1(f) show the captured screen images created by this module when using Windows Notepad while our system is active. Figures 1(a) and 1(f) were created by analyzing the form of the WM_LBUTTONDOWN message, Figures 1(b) and 1(e) were created by analyzing the form of the WM_KEYDOWN messages, and Figures 1(c) and 1(d) were created by analyzing the form of the WM_MENUSELECT messages.

In these images, the target window or object is highlighted, and the click position is displayed by the cursor image if the operation is a mouse action.

B. Publish Module

This module runs on a Web server. On the top page, all the images sent from the storage module are displayed as thumbnails. To switch to the slideshow mode, the user simply clicks on one of the thumbnails. In the slideshow mode, there are backward and forward link buttons that permit users to navigate between images. In the highlighted part of the operation target, users can immediately identify the changed parts. The cursor image and the operation annotations allow the user to identify the targeted operations.

C. Result

We conducted an experiment at a lecture to develop an Android application using the Eclipse development environment. In this lesson, the operations performed by a student to create a project (primarily mouse clicks), the operations used to create an Android Window (primarily click and drag) and the programming instructions (primarily keyboard input) were extracted for use.

Using our system, six students who were late for the lecture reviewed the missed portions of the lesson and attempted to catch up with the instructor's ongoing explanation. All of these students completed these missed operations, and were able to operate their PCs in tandem with their instructor's operations.

D. Discussion

When the pace of the instructor's explanation increases, the number of students who will be unable to follow the operations also increases. In this class, the instructor paced the lecture while periodically checking to ensure that all the students completed the operations in tandem with the presentation. To confirm the operations of students, we recorded the operation process. Checking the operations performed by students after the lecture, we found that a few students could not smoothly perform the drag operations. More specifically, even though the students observed the screen captures and identified the target object, they could not identify the drag destination from the screen capture, and had to click the forward link displayed by the Web browser to obtain that information.

However, once they became familiar with the system, the students realized they could quickly click forward to the next image to determine the drag destination, and then click back to the image displaying the mouse drag operation itself.

Next, we will discuss the times taken for the operation. In the lecture, since explanations are given as the operations are performed, the process takes longer than simply performing the actual operations. However, since there is no waiting time for students who perform operations while observing the operation manual created by the system, there were situations where some students finished the required operations more quickly than the students that simply listened to the lecture.

IV. Conclusion

In this paper, we report on a newly developed system that automatically creates an operation manual based on instructor PC operations that students can watch in real time during lectures, and which can be quickly reviewed by late arriving students. Using our system, the students who were late for the lecture reviewed the missed portions of the lesson and attempted to catch up with the instructor's ongoing explanation. All students successfully completed these missed operations, and were able to operate their PCs in tandem with their instructor's operations.

However, since the experiment described in this paper involved only a limited number of subjects and student participants, it will be necessary to apply the system to additional classes with larger numbers of participating students in future studies in order to more fully confirm its effectiveness.

ACKNOWLEDGMENT

This work was supported by the Japan Society for the Promotion of Science (JSPS) KAKENHI Grant Number 16K16324.

REFERENCES

[1] H. Bandoh, Y. Otsuki, and S. Sawada, "Prototyping of an educational supporting tool to ease instruction of software operation; automatic display of operation process and result," IPSJ SIG Technical Report, pp.1-8, 2003.

[2] T. Itamiya, K Tagawa, and H. Chiyokura, "Development of the Lecture recording system for Superimposing a Blackboard Writing and Lecturer's image on the Lecturer's PC Screen," Japan Society for Educational Technology, pp.119–128, 2011.

[3] "Click! Recorder," 2014, [Online] Available from: http://www.gluesoft.co.jp/en/ClickRec2 [accessed December 2018]

[4] "iTutor," 2018, [Online] Available from: https://itutor.jp/ [accessed December 2018]

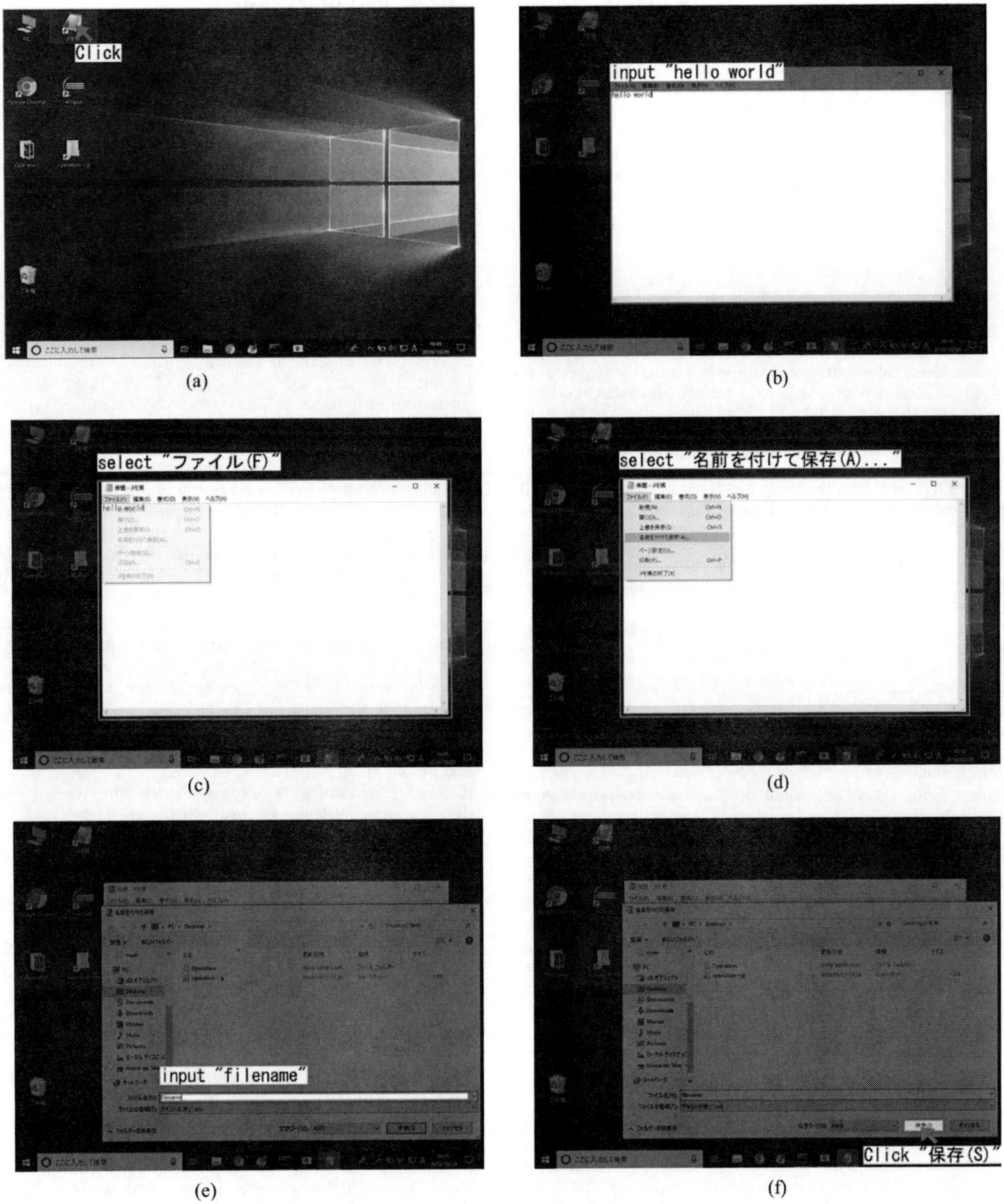

Figure 1. Sample images created by our system based on instructor operation.

Multi-Level Image Presentation Method to Quickly Know Operation Processes of Students for Finding Erroneous Operation

Kenta Morita
Graduate School of Engineering
Mie University
Mie, Japan
Email: k-morita@ip.elec.mie-u.ac.jp

Haruhiko Takase
Graduate School of Engineering
Mie University
Mie, Japan
Email: takase@elec.mie-u.ac.jp

Naoki Morita
Graduate School of Information and
Telecommunication Engineering
Tokai University
Tokyo, Japan
Email: morita@tokai.ac.jp

***Abstract*—In this paper, we developed a system that helps teachers to identify the erroneous operations of a student in computer literacy classes quickly. We considered two requirements for the system: (1) recording all operations, and (2) providing summarized information according to teacher's requests. For the first requirement, the system records screen image for all operations that are acquired by global hook events. For the second requirement, we proposed the multi-level image presentation method. First, all captured images are grouped hierarchically according to their contents. Then, teachers browse captured images by controlling the level of grouped images. Consequently, they reduce the number of images to be confirmed and find erroneous operations quickly. We confirmed the effectiveness of the proposed method through the experiment. Subjects try to find erroneous operations from more than 700 images. Subjects using the proposed method decreased the time for finding erroneous operations by 60%.**

Keywords–Compute-assisted instruction; Operation Process

I. Introduction

Recently, classes in which students use their personal computers are spreading. For classes of a freshman in college, students do some kind of work, programming, writing a report and so on, by using their computers according to a teacher's guide. Some students cannot do the same operation as the guide by the teacher and sometimes cause undesired results. Since students do not understand operations enough, they cannot be aware of erroneous operations, which are causes of undesired results. They would be aware that something was wrong, only after being aware of an undesired result. But they cannot identify the erroneous operation since they did many operations before the undesired result and they believe that their operations were correct. So, they would be confused and ask for help to the teacher. The teacher identifies the erroneous operation by inquiring the operations or by his/her experience. Identifying by inquiring would be hard for the teacher since the student was already confused. So, teachers want to retrace operations to the erroneous operation with a supporting system.

To retrace students' operations, some supporting systems were developed. They record students' operations and provide the teacher with the recorded operations. For example, some methods recording the screen of the student in video format and finding the operation process by seeing the video have been proposed [1]-[3]. By using these methods, the teacher can know all operations that the student performed. However, the teacher would waste time by using these methods, because it is necessary to confirm the video regardless of presence or absence of student's operation. There are several methods that capture the screen each time a student operates, rather than always recording [4][5]. The teacher can know the operation process of the student by confirming the captured images one by one. However, since most captured operations are correct operations, looking at all the operations takes time to identify the erroneous operation. To reduce the time for checking student's operations, it is necessary to reduce the number of images that the teacher checks furthermore. On the other hand, reducing the number of images would cause the shortage of information to identify the erroneous operations. The shortage would be serious for Teaching Assistant(TAs) who are not familiar with the operation to identify the erroneous operation by only seeing the limited operations. So, it is necessary both to record all operations and to easily detect

In this paper, we describe a system to helps teachers identify the erroneous operations of the student quickly. The system records all operations and provides the operations so as to be grasped by them quickly. Recording all operations is similar to the one from [5], and quickness for grasping is done by providing hierarchically grouped operations. If the teacher wants to grasp the operation process roughly, the he/she checks the images containing only the main operations. Also, the teacher looks at all the images if the teacher wants to grasp the operations in detail. By using this method, the teacher can quickly grasp the student's operation process without missing the operations and can identify the erroneous operations of the student as soon as possible.

This paper contains the following flow. Section II describes the method underlying the proposed method. In Section III, we consider how to present the operation information. We discuss the effectiveness of our proposed method in Section IV. Section V presents the conclusion and future work.

II. Previous Method Using Global Hook

This section briefly describes the student's screen recording method which is one of the previous methods using a global hook [4]. This method detects students' operations, captures the screen of the student each time the student operates and provides captured images in order to the teacher.

To detect the student's operation, a mechanism called the global hook, which is provided by an operating system is used. The global hook can intercept messages sent by the operating system to an application. Messages intercepted by the global hook include messages generated by a keyboard or a mouse. These messages are sent at the moment each event occurs.

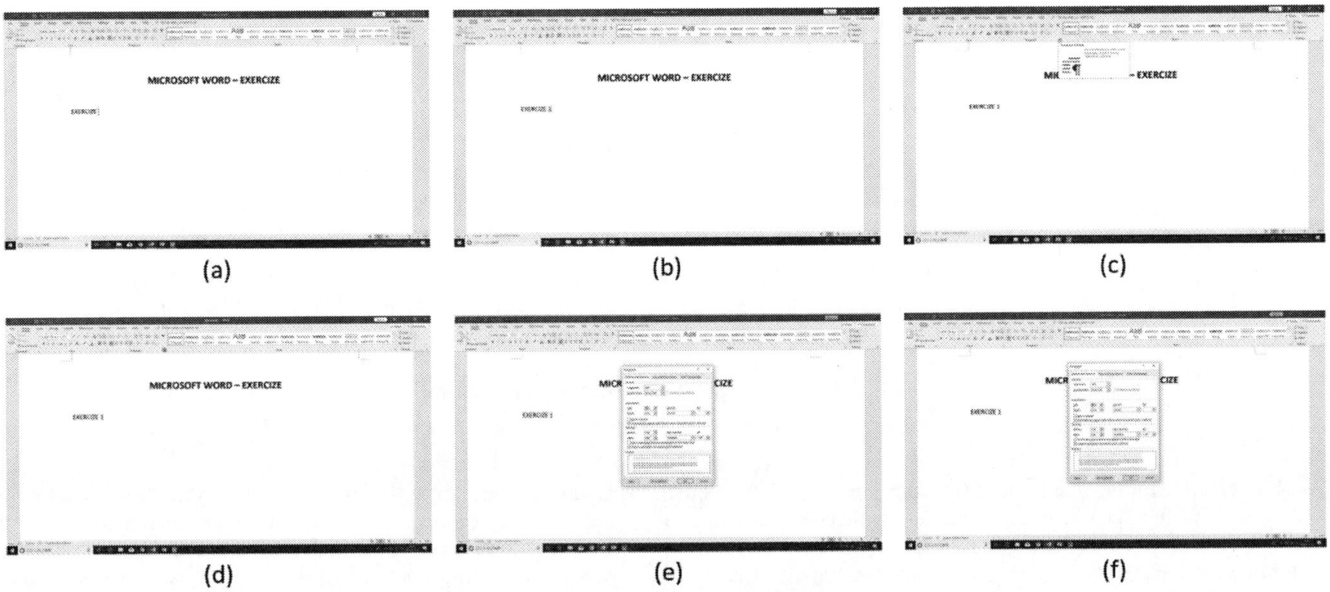

Figure 1. A sample of display by the global hook.
(a) Pressing [space] key, (b) Pressing [1] key, (c) Pressing left click, (d) Releasing left click, (e) Pressing left click, (f) Releasing left click

This method captures the screen when a user's operation is acquired with the global hook. Thereby, the operation process of the student is accumulated in the student's computer as some images.

The captured images are sorted and are provided to the teacher. When the teacher wants to confirm the operation process of the student, he/she sees the captured images one by one in order. By confirming the captured images, the teacher can guess the student's operation. Figure 1 shows images captured by the previous method, arranged in alphabetical order. By looking at these images in order, the teacher finds that the student inputs a sentence, then operates a menu with the mouse, and opens a dialog box.

By knowing the operation process of the student, the teacher can identify the erroneous operations. However, this method has a problem in that it is necessary to confirm all images captured between the moment students started operating and the moment the teacher was asked for help.

III. Proposal

In this section, we propose a method that groups operations hierarchically. With the proposal, the system provides fewer images than the previous system without reducing captured images. As a result, teachers should identify erroneous operations quickly.

The proposed system makes groups from all captured images. In the lowest level (level 0), each group consists of one captured image, which represents one student's operation. In the higher level (level n), each group is a series of some groups of the level below (level n-1) and represents a meaningful operation. The representative image of each group is the last captured image in the group.

The proposed system provides grouped images hierarchically. First, the system shows representative images of the groups only at the highest level. The teacher grasps the student's operations roughly and identifies the group to be focused. Then, the system shows representative images of the groups in the below level of the focused group. The teacher narrows the area to be focused. The teacher repeat them until he/she identifies the erroneous operation.

With the proposed system, teachers can identify the student's erroneous operation quickly, since they can concentrate only on a subset of images. And they do not miss the erroneous operation since they can look all captured images if necessary.

The effectiveness of the proposed system is decided by the rule for grouping. The rule should be decided by the application, target students and target teachers. Here, we show an example for Microsoft Word. When working in Microsoft Word, this method intercepts mouse and keyboard messages given to the operating system. Because messages in software can not be intercepted by proposed system in current state of the art, groups operations similar to messages in software from keyboard and mouse messages. In level 0, each group consists of only one captured image. In level 1, each group consists of a series of groups of level 0 images that represent a primitive operation: typing a word, operating a keyboard short-cut, clicking/double clicking a left/right button of a mouse, and so on. Typing a word is identified by the sequence of key inputs except for space or enter key. Clicking the left mouse button is identified by pressing/releasing event of the left button of the mouse. Other operations are grouped in the same manner. In level 2, each group consists of a series of groups of level 1 that represent a more-abstracted operation: typing a sentence, a combination of keyboard short-cut, selecting a menu by the mouse, and so on.

Figure 2 illustrates the grouping result for Microsoft Word in Japanese. These were taken at the time of writing a report in Japanese. From the level 0 to 1, the first (typing a character) to the third (typing enter key) images in the level 0 are grouped

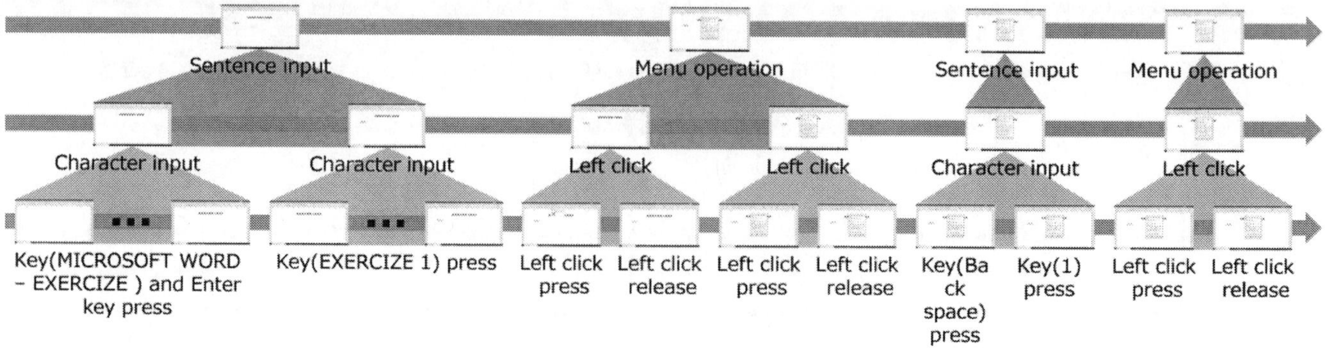

Figure 2. A sample of multi-level image presentation.

as character input. And the fifth (pressing the left mouse button) and the sixth (releasing the left mouse button) images are grouped as left clicking. From the level 1 to 2, the first (character input) and the second (character input) images in the level 1 are grouped as typing a sentence. And the third (left clicking) and the fourth (left clicking) images in the level 1 are grouped as operating a menu.

When browsing the results shown in Figure 2, the system provides images of level 2 first. Then, a teacher selects an image on level 2. Then the system shows images on level 1 that are components of the selected image. And the system shows images on level 0 in the same manner if necessary.

IV. Experiments

In this section, we compare the proposed method with the previous method and confirm the effectiveness. We

A. Experimental Setup

Our aim is that teachers can quickly find an erroneous operation of student. To confirm the effectiveness, we measured the time that it takes testing subjects to find an erroneous operation and compared the case using the proposed method with the case using the previous method. The number of subjects is six. We explained only the contents of the exercise to the subjects. And we asked them to identify the operation error without informing the contents of the operation error. Subjects confirmed the operation process in Microsoft Word exercise. The content of the exercise in this Microsoft Word is preparation of materials, there are operations such as text input, size of letters, typeface change and indent adjustment. The images presented to the subjects were prepared by reproducing the operation error when the student made a mistake in selecting the item in the dialog box before. The operation recorded in this experiment corresponds from the start of the exercise to the student himself made an operation mistake. There are 744 recorded operations, and the erroneous operation is in the 725th. The content of the erroneous operation was to select First line instead of selecting Hanging. The number of captured images was 744, and the number of images presented at each level of the proposed method is shown in Table I.

B. Result

We divided subjects in half and asked each group to discover operation errors by either proposed method or previous method. The table II shows the average time it takes for the subjects to specify the operation mistake when using the proposed method or using the previous method. Comparing the two average times, we found that, in the case of the proposed method, the subjects identified erroneous operation in about half the time of the case of the previous method. We got the following comments from the subjects.

- Even for the TA, who is not familiar with the operation to the application, it is possible to grasp the point where the operation error is likely to be somehow. There is a possibility that he can also find a mistake by looking closely around the point which is likely to be bad.
- In the previous method, it is hard to find an operation mistake because there are a lot of images to be confirmed.

We observed how to check captured images of the subject. As a result, we found that the subjects confirmed the image in order from the image of the operation start regardless of the method. The subjects confirmed the images one by one and grasped the operation process of the student. And, when the subjects found an image when an operation error occurred, they re-examined the previous image and found an erroneous operation.

In the case of the proposed method, the subjects used high level display to grasp the operation process roughly, when the subjects found an image when an operation error occurred, they used low level display and found an erroneous operation. From this, we fathomed that subjects could roughly grasp the operation process of student even using the proposed method. Since the proposed method can present the image of

TABLE I. Number of images presented by the proposed method.

Display level	*Number of presented images*
Level 3	255
Level 2	288
Level 1	744

TABLE II. Time taken to identify erroneous operation.

Method	*Average time(s)*
Proposed method	167.3
Previous method	284.6

the moment the student erroneously operated earlier than the previous method by using the high level display, it is possible to quickly find the erroneous operation.

From these considerations, we can affirm that the proposed image display method is effective.

V. Conclusion

In this paper, we developed a system that helps teachers identify the erroneous operations of the student quickly. We considered two requirements for the system: (1) recording all operations, and (2) providing summarized information according to teacher's requests. For the first requirement, the system records screen images for all operations that are acquired by global hook events. For the second requirement, we proposed the multi-level image presentation method. First, all captured images are grouped hierarchically according to their contents. Then, teachers browse captured images by controlling the level of grouped images. Consequently, the system reduces the number of images to be confirmed and find erroneous operations quickly. In the future, we will try to increase global hook events: not only keyboard and mouse operations but also other types of information, and discuss strategies for grouping captured images.

The recording system has privacy concerns. For that reason, we will implement recording on / off in the future and investigate how the student's behavior, such as whether the student can install this system, is affected.

References

[1] G. Thavamalar, "Successful implementation of e-learning: Pedagogical considerations", The internet and higher education, Vol.4 No.3, pp.287-299.

[2] R. Stannard, "Screen capture software for feedback in language education", Second International Wireless Ready Symposium, MAR. 2008, pp. 16-20, ISSN 1995-4557.

[3] J. Nigel, P. Georghiades, and J. Gunson, "Student feedback via screen capture digital video: Stimulating student's modified action", Higher Education Vol.64 No.5, pp.593-607.

[4] N. Morita, "A Programming Process Visualization System With Global Hooking", Society for Information Technology and Teacher Education(SITE2014), MAR. 2014, pp. 1945- 1953, ISBN 978-1-939797-07-0.

[5] K. Morita, H. Takase and N. Morita, "Method for Quick Identification of Computer Operations Performed by a Student", The Ninth International Conference on Mobile, Hybrid, and On-line Learning, MAR. 2017, pp. 90- 93, ISBN 978-1-61208-541-8.

Exploring Aspects of a Faculty Digital Learning Channel: The Case of Eclips

Ilke Franquet, Christine Lippens
Kelly Martens and Herwig Mannaert

Faculty of Business and Economics
University of Antwerp
Email: {ilke.franquet,herwig.mannaert}@uantwerp.be

***Abstract*—In recent years, video tutorials have become an important tool to enhance active student learning. They are considered to be an effective and efficient instrument to enhance the progression of students. In 2016, the Faculty of Business and Economics of the University of Antwerp formulated a vision on technology-enhanced learning, with a strong focus on the creation and the use of both course specific and integrative video tutorials. To make the tutorials available to students throughout their entire study career, the faculty started in 2017 with the development of a faculty-wide learning channel, called Eclips. The platform offers students the opportunity to prepare for a lecture, revise learning content and fill knowledge gaps across the curriculum. Besides enhancing the pedagogical project by means of the student channel, (sub)channels were defined in 2018 for two additional target groups: the pre-students and the alumni. This enables the channel to support two other aspects of the academic mission of a faculty: the dissemination of knowledge and the interaction with the broader environment.**

Keywords–Technology Enhanced Learning; Blended learning; Digital learning channels.

I. Introduction

The importance of digital learning material has grown in recent years. The university and in particular the faculties Faculty of Business Economics (FBE) and Faculty of Medicine and Health Sciences (FMHS) focused on video tutorials used in education to address the heterogeneous incoming and ongoing students and to improve knowledge across the curriculum. The existing video tutorials were selected by the lecturers to make sure that the quality and the level were aligned with the final objectives of the programmes. These videos were used during the course or served to clarify certain topics of the course. Lecturers could also create their own videos in the recording rooms that have been available on the different campuses of the university.

However, there was no platform available to collect, group, and structure all this information. Therefore, the business and economics faculty decided to create a digital learning channel in order to provide the students and lecturers with a clear structure, where they can easily navigate through all the content that the students have learnt during their bachelor and master years. By creating the *Eclips Learning Channel*, the faculty wants to give the students the possibility to revise at their own pace and to consult educational video material (also used in previous study years) when they feel it is necessary to do so. It also gives lecturers a complete view on the study material that students are supposed to know.

In this paper, we use a case-based approach, based on the Eclips learning channel, to explore several key aspects of designing and organizing such a faculty digital learning channel. In Section 2, we give a brief literature overview of the possible power of video as a teaching medium, and present the way that the faculty decided to leverage this technology. The actual structure, content, and design of the Eclips Learning Channel is detailed Section 2. Section 4 gives an overview of the main realizations thus far, and presents the current and future efforts to broaden the reach of the learning channel. Finally, we present some conclusions in Section 5.

II. Academic Video Tutorials

A. The Case for Video Tutorials

Apart from the great advantage of flexibility, video can be a very powerful teaching medium, as stated by Thomson et al.[1]. Video tutorials, often presented as screencasts, are short videos adopted by lecturers to stimulate active learning during the course. In the form of shorter mini-lectures, explanations of assignments or exam solutions, they can be used as supplementary resources when teaching a module [2]. Research, for instance by Morris and Chikwa [3], has confirmed that students prefer short screencasts that summarise lectures or delve in-depth into complex concepts. Lloyd and Robertson demonstrated positive learning gains in an undergraduate statistics course for students using a supplemental video tutorial [4].

Apart from being part of the lecturer's own module, video tutorials can also be used to cope with the heterogeneity of a student group by offering students the opportunity to refresh knowledge or to fill up knowledge gaps. Research by Pinder-Grover et al. showed that screencasts lead to demonstrable improvements in course performance, especially for those who enter with the least amount of exposure to the subject matter [5]. These hiatus frequently occur at the beginning of a study career, because of lack of background in a certain topic due to limited prior knowledge when entering university. Moreover, it is also manifest that students continuously need to refresh specific topics during their studies because of the inevitable process of knowledge evaporation.

B. Faculty Vision on Video Learning

At the Faculty of Business and Economics of the University of Antwerp, video tutorials tended to be part of a certain module, incorporated in the related Blackboard course only. To make video tutorials available for students during their entire study career, the faculty set up a digital learning channel with permanent and mobile access. Students can watch the tutorials during their studies whenever they need to. Lecturers can refer to this channel in a cross-curriculum way.

The faculty has organised its courses based on so-called *Learning Tracks*, and leverages this structure to deal with various aspects or cross-cutting concerns of academic courses, such as internationalisation and examination forms [6]. Therefore, the digital *Learning Channel ECLIPS*, is being organised around these learning tracks: Business Economics, Economics, Quantitative Methods, Engineering, Information Systems, Business Communication, Research Methods and Broadening Subjects. The faculty also decided to adopt an hybrid model for its video tutorials, using both in-house produced tutorials and existing clips from external providers. The channel was implemented at the start of the academic year 2017-2018, and launched for first-year undergraduate students, i.e., first bachelor year. The main emphasis was on providing resources for this group of students. In 2018-2019, the focus moved towards the second bachelor year.

In order to support and encourage in-house made video tutorials, the faculty set up its own ECLIPS recording studio. When developing a video tutorial, different video production styles are offered to lecturers by the production team, such as screencasts and recording with glassboard or green screen. It is important to provide a variety in video production styles as standardisation of video production faces many limitations, as stated for instance by Hansch et al.: *It is important to match the video style to the instructor. There is not a one-size-fits-all approach* [7]. For the sourcing of the videos from elsewhere, the faculty relies upon their faculty staff to assess the quality and consistency of the selected videos. A quality checklist and a list of guidelines were developed to evaluate both in-house made and external videos.

III. The Eclips Learning Channel

In this section, we detail the actual development of the learning channel, including three main aspects: structure, content and design. But first, we discuss the approach to set up the concept, and gather people around it.

A. Approach

First of all, lecturers who showed interest in Digital and Blended Learning and Teaching (DBLT) before, were contacted to ask for input on the content of the learning channel. In order to ensure that the entire faculty was represented, these lecturers were spread across the various departments. Moreover, the content of the learning channel was discussed on the various department meetings. All this information was collected in order to get a good overview on the information that lecturers believed to be necessary for their own course. Since the students are the main target group, a workshop was organized in which a group of 21 students were asked to give their opinion on the structure, content and design of this learning channel. This feedback was taken into account during the further development of Eclips.

As with other pedagogical aspects or so-called cross-cutting concerns, the structure is based on the eight learning tracks within the faculty [6]. The project was initially defined for a three year period, during which the faculty envisioned to add content gradually. During the creation of the learning channel, extra attention was given to the visual or graphical aspect of Eclips. To make adoption of the learning channel a success, the two target groups — students and lecturers — needed to be reached, informed and actively stimulated. As stated before, the focus during the first academic year was on the courses of the first year bachelor. Therefore, the main target group initially consisted of the first year's students who were informed in the information sessions at the beginning of the academic year. In their welcome package, they received for instance a pen with the Eclips logo. For the adoption by other students (Bachelor 2, Bachelor 3, Masters) the faculty is counting on the second target group to spread the word. This second group, the lecturers, was informed during the yearly meeting in the beginning of the academic year. They were also invited to take a look at the recording room containing the necessary supporting equipment to record video tutorials.

B. Structure

The learning channel is embedded in Blackboard and has a clear structure to navigate, both for students and lecturers. The Eclips Learning Channel presents video tutorials and digital modules according to the structure of the eight learning tracks within the curriculum. Each learning track decides on and defines their own substructure by mutual agreement within the learning track. Mindmaps are used to guide the students and lecturers throughout this structure.

The technology behind the channel structure is quite elementary and consists of two basic building blocks: the electronic learning platform Blackboard and a PowerPoint presentation to represent the mindmap structure, which is converted into a HTML5-package within Blackboard. The Eclips Learning Channel is made available in the list of courses within Blackboard, which is accessible to all students and lecturers of the faculty. Opposed to other courses, the learning channel will be visible during the entire academic life of both the student and lecturer. When the student or lecturer clicks on Eclips in Blackboard, he is presented with the main HTML5-mindmap of Figure 1. When navigating to a video

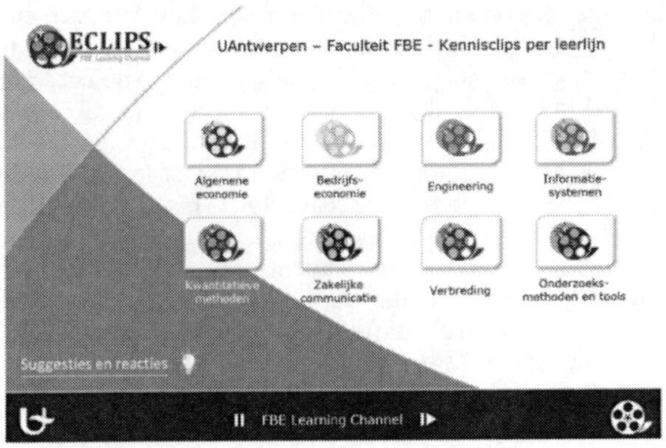

Figure 1. Main structure of the mindmap.

in the mindmap, an information sheet shows details about the author, the production date and duration of the video, the used platform or source, and a short description of the video content. Each information sheet has a unique identifier that refers to the video tutorial or digital module. The video starts by clicking on the play button in the right corner of this information sheet, as represented in Figure 2. Hyperlinks

Figure 2. Example information sheet.

behind the icons in the mindmap ensure that the user can navigate through the different learning tracks to find the video tutorial or digital module he or she wants to consult. The technology used to create the HTML5-package ensures that users are able to navigate through the mindmaps and watch the videos on their mobile devices, a concern that was expressed during a workshop organized with the students.

In case a student has a suggestion to upload a video tutorial in the learning channel, or there is an error in the video tutorial, the student can contact the Eclips team through an interactive forum. Thanks to the unique identifier in the information sheet, the student can easily refer to the video tutorial.

C. Content

In the first academic year of the project, 2017-2018, the faculty focused on courses for the first year bachelor students. More specifically, the focus was on the courses with a low pass rate and the courses taken by a high number of students, i.e., Accountancy, Economics, Mathematics and Statistics. The lecturers of these subjects received technical support from the Eclips team members to create the video tutorials, which benefits the content in general and especially the pace at which the content of the learning channel is created. Even though these four subjects receive priority, other subjects are also invited to create video tutorials. In the second academic year, 2018-2019, the focus shifted to the courses of the second year bachelor, in order to finish the project in 2019-2020 with a focus on the third year bachelor. This time path ensures that the content of the learning channel gradually grows in a synchronous way with the students who started their academic life at the same time the learning channel was launched. The students can consult the learning channel during their entire academic career at the University of Antwerp.

The content of Eclips consists of both existing videos and in-house made videos. The existing videos are carefully selected by the lecturers, keeping the quality of the video tutorials in mind. These are video tutorials from websites like *Khan Academy* and *PatrickJMT*. The faculty provides a recording studio where lecturers can record video tutorials with the assistance of an Eclips team member. Various types of recordings are possible in order to realize a variety of content in the learning channel. Examples of these types are video tutorials making use of a glassboard, handwritten video tutorials, PowerPoint presentations, and green screen recordings. The type of the recording depends on the preference of the lecturer and the topic of the video tutorial. The current number of available video tutorials for each learning track is shown in Table 1, and will be discussed in the next section.

D. Design

The visual aspect certainly plays a crucial role in encouraging students and lecturers to make systematic use of this video platform. Together with the graphical design team of the University of Antwerp, a logo, a set of icons, and a house style were designed. The icons are used in the mindmap in which the students navigate through the structure. The logo makes it possible to brand the in-house made video tutorials and the learning channel. Even though Blackboard is the platform that is used for the learning channel, the mindmap, logos and icons give it a refreshing and contemporary look.

Figure 3. Example introduction screen.

In order to be sure that the in-house made videos by the lecturers exhibit a uniform look and feel, the in-house made video tutorials start with the Eclips introduction screen, represented in Figure 3. To provide maximum support, a template for PowerPoint and Camtasia (a video editing program) were created. The main colour used in the templates is green, since this is the colour that represents the faculty. The various learning tracks have different unique colours.

IV. Realizations and Future Plans

A. Content and Usage

A first realization is of course the mere fact that the faculty developed a dedicated, visually attractive learning channel, offering both in-house and external video tutorials and digital modules, and providing a clear structure in which the students can easily navigate. However, the actual realizations need to be expressed in terms of created content and student use of the video tutorials. Table I shows the number of video tutorials and

TABLE I. Number of video tutorials or digital modules in Eclips.

Learning track	In-house	External	Total
Business communication	7	6	13
Research methods and tool	11	10	21
Quantitative methods	43	108	151
Business economics	58	0	58
Economics	15	0	15
Total	**134**	**124**	**258**

digital modules, that were available for each learning track in may 2018, less than one year after the launch of Eclips. Only the learning tracks that contain content are mentioned in Table I. In Figure 4 the growth in the different phases of the project are summarized. This figure shows that especially

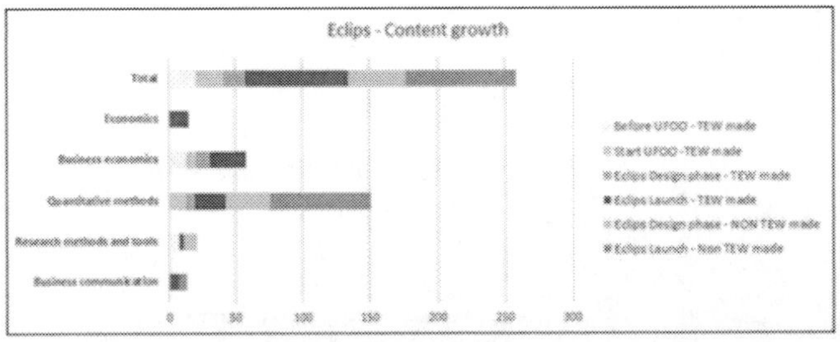

Figure 4. Eclips Content growth.

after the launch of the learning channel, the content in general and the production of in-house made video tutorials started booming. The highest growth rate can be found in the learning track quantitative methods. This is both logical and desirable, since the content of quantitative methods covers the core competences that are needed in other learning tracks.

Through the *Mediasite* of the university, the video platform in which the in-house made videos are uploaded, the lecturers can consult statistics on the views of their video tutorials. It gives an overview of how many students have watched the videos, which parts of the video have been watched the most, etcetera. In other words, it offers the lecturer a clear insight in the topics that students find more relevant and consult accordingly. These results are, up to may 2018 or less than a year after the launch of Eclips, summarized in Table II.

TABLE II. NUMBER OF VIEWS FOR THE VARIOUS VIDEO TUTORIALS.

Learning track	Number clips	Total views	Average views
Business communication	7	269	38
Research methods and tool	11	1232	112
Quantitative methods	43	8140	189
Business economics	58	59327	1023
Economics	15	2639	176
Total	**134**	**71607**	**534**

B. Synergies with Other Faculties

Since the launch of Eclips in 2017, two other faculties of the University of Antwerp started with the implementation of their own tailor-made ECLIPS Learning Channel. These additional faculty channels share the Eclips brand, including the concept and the design, but consist of videos which are specific to the domains offered in the degree programmes of these faculties. This interfaculty cooperation clearly offers multiple opportunities for the future. Such opportunities range from simple economies of scale for recording equipment, to the exchange and co-creation of videos and/or scripts.

The growth of Eclips into multiple subchannels also implies an increase in efforts to manage the Eclips channel(s). For instance, the regulations concerning copyrights should be taken into account. Using video excerpts or short videos as educational resources without adding changes in a protected learning environment is allowed by Belgian legislation. However, referring or linking to the existing tutorials on the external channels should be done very carefully. Moreover, a growing learning channel consisting of three subchannels, needs permanent maintenance and monitoring. Due to the interaction with different parties delivering videos, this may become quite challenging.

C. Reaching Multiple Target Groups

It is part of a university mission to connect and interact with the outside world. In 2018, the faculty included the pre-students as second target group for the in-house produced tutorials. Three public subchannels were launched for pupils of secondary school and their teachers, in the domains of mathematics, statistics and accountancy. The tutorials are offered to provide this new target group with a tool to bridge possible knowledge gaps between secondary school and university before entering university. As such, these tutorials will help pre-students to assess their readiness, and function as a support instrument in their study orientation process.

As lifelong learning becomes and remains a crucial issue in our society, the faculty recently decided to address alumni as a third target group of the ECLIPS Learning Channel. Specialized expert knowledge, based on research being done by academics, will be transformed into video tutorials as well, serving both graduate students and alumni. Unlike the more accessible knowledge offered in the subchannel for pre-students, more advanced niche knowledge is targeted for the alumni subchannel. This channel is yet to be launched formally, but initial preparations have already begun.

Figure 5 presents a schematic overview of the various Eclips (sub)channels, based on the corresponding target groups, i.e., pre-students, students, and alumni. For every target group, the technological hosting platform and the type of content are included in the summary. As an illustration, the QR codes referencing the pre-student channels are also included.

V. CONCLUSIONS

The development of the Eclips Learning Channel proofs that a faculty can indeed build an efficient digital learning channel with limited human, i.e., three part time team members, and technological resources, i.e., Blackboard and PowerPoint. As the channel has only been launched a little more than one year ago, it would be premature to draw any hard conclusions about its added value and efficacy. An enquiry with both students and lecturers about the structure, the content and the design of the video tutorials is currently being organized.

However, based on the registrated viewing statistics, we can already cautiously say that the learning channel is gaining momentum. Moreover, we are able to conclude that students consult the video tutorials more often when the lecturer explicitly refers to them. As the learning channel offers a better overview across various topics of the different courses, we expect that the learning channel will have a positive impact on the study process of the students, and the productive interaction between students and lecturers.

A clear indication of the (perceived) added value is that the Faculty of Medicine and Health Sciences, decided to replicate

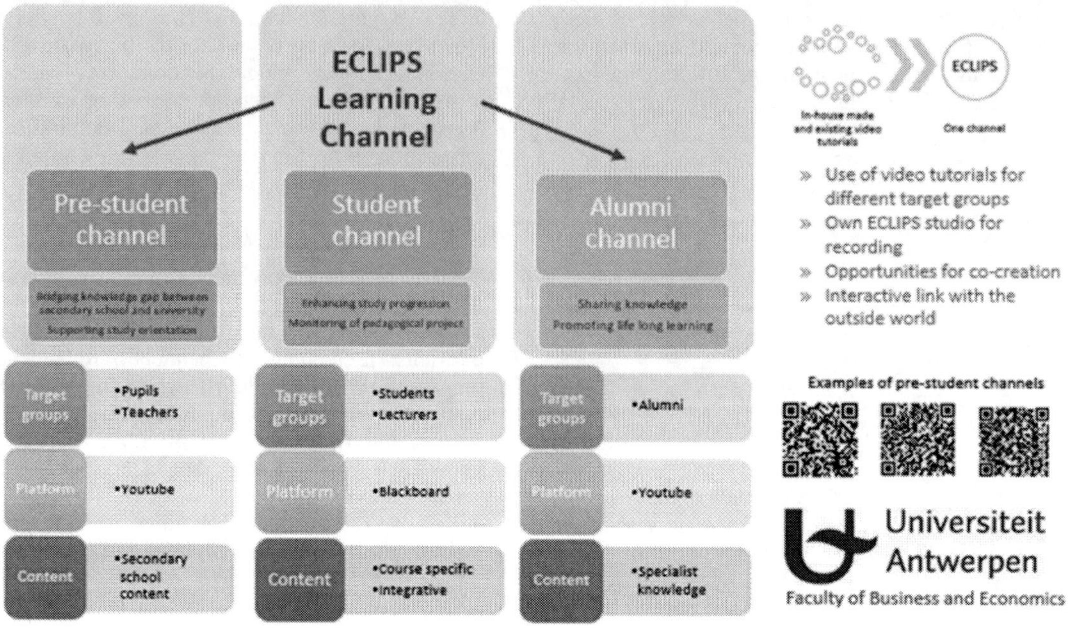

Figure 5. Schematic representation of Eclips (sub)channels and various target groups.

the entire concept of the Eclips learning channel, and adapted the mindmaps to make a logical structure for their own faculty.

REFERENCES

[1] A. Thomson, R. Bridgstock, and C. Willems, "'Teachers flipping out' beyond the online lecture: maximising the educational potential of video." Journal of Learning Design, vol. 7, no. 3, 2014, pp. 67–78.

[2] M. Lee, S. Pradhan, and B. Dangarno, "The effectiveness of screencasts and cognitive tools as scaffolding for novice object-oriented programmers." Journal of Information Technology Education, vol. 7, 2008, pp. 61–80.

[3] C. Morris and C. Gladson, "Screencasts: How effective are they and how do students engage with them? Active learning in higher education," Teaching of Psychology, vol. 15, no. 1, 2012, pp. 25–37.

[4] S. Lloyd and C. L. Robertson, "Screencast Tutorials Enhance Student Learning of Statistics," Teaching of Psychology, vol. 39, no. 1, 2012, pp. 67–71.

[5] K. Green, T. Pinder-Grover, and J. Millunchick, "Impact of Screencast Technology: Connecting the Perception of Usefulnes and the Reality of Performance." Journal of Engineering Education, vol. 4, 2012, pp. 717–737.

[6] G. Oorts, H. Mannaert, P. De Bruyn, and I. Franquet, On the evolvable and traceable design of (under)graduate education programs. Springer International Publishing, 2016, vol. 252, pp. 86–100.

[7] H. Hansch, L. Hillers, K. McConachie, C. Newman, P. Schmidt, and T. Schildhauer, "The Role of Video in Online Learning: Findings From the Field and Critical Reflections." p. 32, 2015.

Survey on Intelligent Dialogue in e-Learning Systems

Felix G. Hamza-Lup
Computer Science
College of Engineering and Computing
Georgia Southern University
Savannah, Georgia, USA
e-mail: fhamzalup@georgiasouthern.edu

Ioana R. Goldbach
Center for Research and Studies in Management and Marketing
Valahia University of Targoviste
Targoviste, Dambovita, Romania
e-mail: ioana.goldbach@icstm.ro

Abstract— **Ever since ancient times, learning was a two-way process, a dialogue among the tutor and the learner. The transfer of knowledge implies social interaction, hence the dialogue is of utmost importance. With the widespread of social media and mobile systems, learners expect quick, easy responses to their questions any time of the day. As e-Learning systems promote time and location flexibility, synchronous dialogue in such systems should not be bound to the time frames that the instructor is available, but should allow learners active real-time feedback throughout the day. Such synchronous interaction is possible through a variety of tools like: automated intelligent grading, intelligent tutoring systems and intelligent facilitator agents embedded in the Learning Management System or social networks. This paper provides an overview of automated dialogue characteristics and a survey on recent research efforts in academia and industry in building intelligent dialogue capable systems. Imagine a system that adapts intelligently to learners' requests and allows them to take control of their own learning, making the bulky learning interface transparent to the user.**

Keywords-adaptive chatbots; intelligent user interfaces; artificial intelligence; adaptive dialogue.

I. INTRODUCTION

Generation Z, the first generation after Millennials, is defined as people born from the mid-1990s to the early 2000s makes up approximate 25% of the U.S. population, making them a larger cohort than the Baby Boomers or Millennials [1][2]. The young generation is very comfortable with technology, and keen on using mobile devices in their daily routine. They want their learning to be personalized to meet their needs while still enabling collaboration with their peers and mentors. Learning on the move, using mobile devices and liberated from a static classroom environment such learners still require the face-to-face-like traditional classroom interaction.

Due to the increase of multimedia content on the web, and deeper penetration of machine learning into various applications, it is possible to deploy adaptive systems that guide student learning at the users' request. While multimedia is gaining popularity on the Web with many technologies that support animation, video, audio and even novel forms of haptic (i.e., tactile) interaction [3], unconstrained use of multimedia results in user interfaces that confuse users and makes it harder for them to understand the information [4]. To cope with the amount of information available online, the dialogue has to be adaptively managed based on the user's requirements and level of knowledge [5]. Adaptive dialogues can be implemented through Artificial Intelligence (AI) supported active assistants (e.g., chat bots) and other intelligent tutoring systems [6]. Such automated systems respond to natural language requests, provide answers and learn in this process. Building on the data they acquire about the users' requests, they can make suggestions, adapt information to the users' needs, and simulate an instructor.

While the course content is important, the content exchanged through the teacher and learner's dialogue (synchronous and asynchronous) is the most important component in the e-Learning environment [7], even for hybrid courses approaches [8][9].

The paper is structured as follows. Section 2 provides a brief overview of synchronous/asynchronous tools for dialogue support followed in Section 3 by a brief review of intelligent, adaptive dialogue with a tutoring agent. Section 4 provides a survey on recent intelligent automated facilitators, including the avatar forms in Virtual Reality/Mixed Reality (VR/MR) environments. Near future trends are discussed in the conclusion.

II. INTELLIGENT DIALOGUE IN E-LEARNING

A new study [10], indicates that over 80% of high school students use smartphones regularly, while 90% of the students agree that tablets will change the way students learn in the very near future and more than 80% of them agree that using tablets in the classroom allows them to optimize their learning. In an effort to cope with these fast technological advances, a continuous improvement of course materials and adaptation to the mobile devices is required but not sufficient. Generating intelligent dialogue among the users of an e-Learning system becomes a challenge. Moreover, dialogue becomes itself the central piece of learning as the lack of dialogue usually is associated with the lack of interest in the topic. Research suggests that learning is also enabled from the observation of the dialogue, the reflection induced by the potential of submitting questions and answers, and in the interaction between the face-to-face and on-line environments [11].

Intelligent dialogue is an enabling discussion allowing the learner to advance his/her understanding of concepts and paradigms associated with a specific paradigm. Such dialogue may be established between the learner and the following types of tutors:

- *Instructor* – in a synchronous or asynchronous session, where the instructor is the main decision factor in providing learning directions to the learner.
- *Peer* – refers to the peers of the leaner (i.e., other learners) that have understood a particular concept or paradigm and are capable of explaining the concept to the learner in a sometimes, more "understandable" way.
- *Intelligent agent.* A software component designed to manage and adapt to the learner's requirements and background knowledge. Such a software component is usually driven by a machine learning algorithm [12] and it establishes a meaningful dialogue considering the learner's requirements and background.

Regardless of the type of the participants in the dialogue, an e-Learning systems supports different types of communication tools. In case of an intelligent software agent, the integration of the software module with one or more communication tools must be achieved. The communication tools can be divided into synchronous and asynchronous as illustrated in Figure 1, and their use depends on the time availability of the participants.

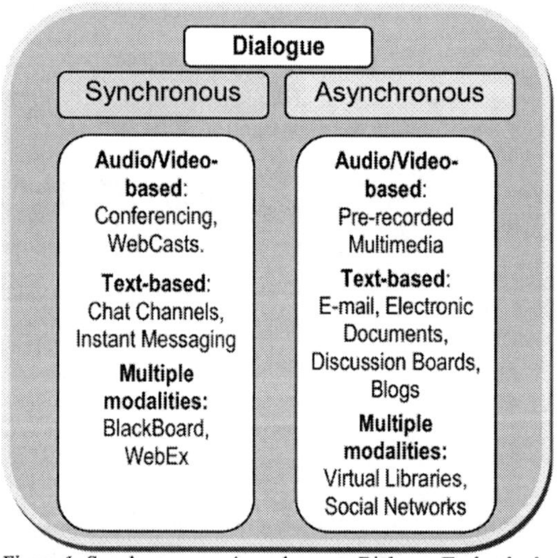

Figure 1. Synchronous vs Asynchronous Dialogue Technologies

A. *Intelligent Synchronous Dialogue*

Synchronous dialogue is an essential component of discussions, lectures and in general presentations that occur at a predefined point in time and are typical in a face-to-face lecture. With the wide spread and proliferation of the Internet, such synchronous dialogue is supported through learning environments that provide multiple ways of interacting, sharing and the ability to ask and answer questions in real-time using synchronous learning technologies. Videoconferencing, web-casts, instant messaging and interactive learning systems supporting chat-based communication are just a few examples.

Synchronous dialogue requires participants to be available at the same time, however there is another essential requirement that is sometimes forgotten: the participants must also have to dedicate similar time frames for dialogue (i.e., class times are often set to 50 minutes intervals). Care must be taken to keep the dialogue from degrading into a monologue.

Techniques to improve synchronous dialogue from the tutor's perspective include: assessing the learners' background knowledge and skills level to predict the capability of the learners to grasp the content and ensure class uniformity; establishing a rapport with the learner at the beginning of the dialogue; High interactivity by keeping text-light and activity-heavy to stimulate the interaction; Encourage the learner to send queries and share his insights; Adapt dialogue pace based on the learner.

On the learner's side, it is important that the learner assumes an active participation role in the dialogue. Furthermore, self-directed motivation is expected of the participants in synchronous dialogue.

B. *Intelligent Asynchronous Dialogue*

An asynchronous dialogue is usually built upon the idea of time flexibility from the participant's perspective. While synchronous dialog requires participant to be online at the same time, asynchronous systems dialogue is usually build on communication systems like e-mail and discussion forums and their various forms under social networks or specialized research networks (e.g., Academia, Research Gate, etc.)

In an asynchronous learning environment learners are encouraged to actively participate in their own learning, providing them the chance to cooperate with their peers, provide peer feedback, and reflect on their personal learning objectives and outcomes. Such an environment implemented through a discussion forum for example and associated with a proper reward grading system, can increase the learner's motivation as well as inter-peer interaction, generating the basis for an intelligent dialog among peers and hence improving the learning outcomes [9][10].

In a web-based client-server environment, even though there are many types of asynchronous applications, communication can be classified as: poll, push, and long-poll [13]. If a parallel is drawn among these categories and the asynchronous dialogue between the tutor and learner, the following dialogue categories are obtained, see Figure 2:

- **Polling, asynchronous dialogue**: the learner asks to the tutor at regular intervals and the tutor responds with guiding information. Such an approach can be implemented for example using an e-mail system with the *"polling"* initiated by the learner.
- **Long-polling, asynchronous dialogue**: is similar with the first approach in that the learner is sending a question to the tutor however the connection is kept open and the tutor provides an answer when s/he has the information available. Interestingly, such asynchronous communication can be implemented thorough a *synchronous* tool (e.g., web-chat) with the

condition that, both the learner and the tutor keep the chat channel open for a long period of time and monitor it for activity.

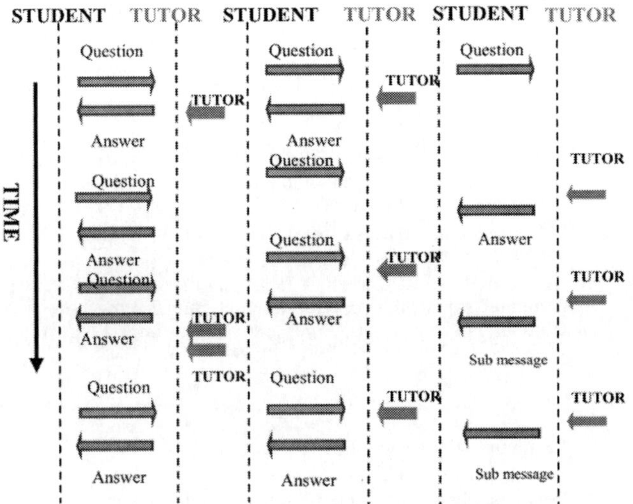

Figure 2. Three approaches: Poll, Long-Poll vs. Push Dialogue

- **Push asynchronous dialogue:** the learner subscribes to a tutor channel by sending an initial request/question and from that point on s/he receives answers/updates *"pushed"* by the tutor. Such a dialogue can be initiated through a subscription to a discussion thread in a discussion forum for example.

III. Intelligent and Adaptive Dialogue

The establishment of an intelligent *dialogue* itself is fundamental, as a simple one-way communication between the tutor and the learner, i.e., a *monologue* is a one way communication channel that eventually requires feedback. Although a monologue is theoretically defined as a "prolonged talk or discourse by a single speaker" conversations between two parties who are not really listening to each other are, essentially, monologues concealed as dialogues. The intelligent, adaptive and automated dialogue attributes have the following meaning:

- *Intelligent* dialogue must reveal good judgment and/or sound thought from both the tutor and learner.
- *Automated* dialogue implies a computing algorithm behind the user interface generating and managing the dialogue (i.e., an intelligent agent) with the learner and augmenting or replacing temporary the real tutor.
- *Adaptive* dialogue implies that various aspects are taken into account (e.g., user's background knowledge and progress) and the tutoring agent is able to adapt to the learner, obviously exhibiting a certain level of intelligence.

Intelligent, automated, adaptive dialogue between a learner and a software tutoring agent may be implemented in a learning management system at different stages:

- *Assessment:* through automated grading that provides the learner with feedback after and assessment (quiz, exam, etc.) has completed. It simulates the behavior of a human tutor, and helps assess learners' knowledge, analyzing their answers, providing feedback and proposing personalized training plans, mostly in an asynchronous context. Automated grading is cheap, quick and without human bias, however it has serious limitations when applied to essay-type content assessment [14].
- *Content Creation: "Smart content" creation*, from digitized guides of textbooks to customizable learning digital interfaces, are being introduced at all levels, from elementary school to corporate environments [6].
- *Content Delivery*: intelligent tutoring systems have seen a tremendous amount of progress in recent years [7]. Recent advances in Artificial Intelligence (AI) have enabled dialogue management frameworks like Artificial Intelligent Dialogue Agent (AIDA) [12].

Integration of intelligent, adaptive and automated dialogue in popular Learning Management Systems (LMS) (e.g., Docebo, Adobe Captive Prime, Desire2Learn, Moodle, Looop, SkillCast, etc.) is still lagging behind. Most LMSs improve interaction through concepts like *gamification,* and enable learner's self-management and enhanced visualization of learning progress, however dialogue is pushed to the peer or tutor level.

IV. Intelligent Automated Facilitators

The main purpose of an automated facilitator in an e-Learning environment is dialogue facilitation for learning. Most facilitator systems rely on speech recognition and/or text analysis and interpretation.

The industry has implemented a variety of natural language ChatBots and voice-recognition modules trough projects like Apple's Siri, Google Now, Microsoft's Cortana, IBM's Watson. LMS environments like Khan Academy, YouTube, Coursera, Lynda, and other massive open online courses (MOOCs) are growing in popularity, however they are still lagging behind in terms of intelligent dialogue creation. Many of these tools suffer from the lack of the immediacy and motivational qualities of personal interaction with a human. However, the effort to improve is ongoing with the goal of powering the intelligent dialogue inside a multitude of devices and digital services (e.g., Viv labs [15]) along the "intelligence becomes a utility" slogan.

Among the notable ongoing research projects in automated, intelligent facilitator's development, Mika [16] provides learners feedback and hints based on the learners' background knowledge and the learner's problem solving strategy. University of Southern California Institute for Creative Technologies is leading for a few decades research efforts in delivering Virtual/Mixed Reality based intelligent *avatars* that act as facilitators for different tasks using the *"Virtual Classroom"* paradigm. The *SimCoach* project [17] for example, implements a virtual human (avatar) support agent that facilitates intelligent dialogue with military personnel and family members to seek information and advice related to their healthcare. Moreover they have expanded the avatar facilitator approach to other areas like: STEM education, CANVAS project [18] and PAL3 [19], a system for delivering education materials and intelligent dialogue via mobile devices, to provide on-the-job training and support lifelong learning.

Projects like TLE TeachLivE™ [20] , reverse the coin, and explore Mixed Reality classrooms with simulated learners that provide tutors the opportunity to develop their pedagogical practice through intelligent dialogue in a safe environment that doesn't place real learners at risk [21]. European Union research efforts (e.g., iTalk2Learn [22]) emphasize the importance of intelligent dialogue through interdisciplinary projects that aggregate expertise from machine learning, user modeling, intelligent tutoring systems, educational psychology and mathematics.

V. Conclusion

The dialogue is an essential component of any human activity, and it is fundamental for any type of interaction. Particularly in education, its importance is amplified by the fact that knowledge transfer occurs in the process of social interaction through intelligent dialogue.

Artificial intelligence has been "*married*" with education for more than 30 years [23]. Personalizing teaching, learning 21st century skills, life-long and life-wide learning will spawn many AI based applications, targeted at new forms of intelligent dialogue design and development involving human senses beyond audio and visual. However care must be taken, to train teachers on how to balance their competences between the new, AI driven, intelligent dialogue systems and the traditional class activities.

Haptic ("tactile") interfaces [24] and Web3D [25] have recently been employed in e-Learning prototypes to enhance intelligent dialogue as well as to widen the communication channel. With the rapid evolution of technology, the 3D and haptic sense, seem poised for immediate adoption into virtual facilitators, embodied like virtual humans, for intelligent dialogue tailored to each learner.

References

[1] K. Dill, "7 Things Employers Should Know About The Gen Z Workforce," Forbes, 2015, URL: https://www.forbes.com/sites/kathryndill/ [accessed: 2019-01-01].

[2] "The Nielsen Total Audience Report: Q1 2017", URL: https://www.nielsen.com/us/en/insights/reports/2017/the-nielsen-total-audience-report-q1-2017.html/ [accessed: 2019-01-07].

[3] F. G. Hamza-Lup and F. A. Kocadag, "Simulating Forces. Learning Through Touch, Virtual Laboratories," Proceedings of the International Conference on Mobile, Hybrid, and Online Learning, Nice, France, Feb. 24, 2013, pp 55-58, IARIA XPS Press, ISBN: 978-1-61208-253-0, URL: https://digitalcommons.georgiasouthern.edu/compsci-facpubs/125/ [accessed: 2019-01-10].

[4] J. Nielsen, "Guidelines for Multimedia on the Web", 1995, URL: https://www.nngroup.com/articles/guidelines-for-multimedia-on-the-web/ [accessed: 2019-01-10].

[5] "Smart Content", URL: https://www.netexlearning.com/en/ [accessed: 2019-01-10].

[6] V. K. Chaudhri, H. C. Lane, D. Gunning, and J. Roschelle, "Intelligent Learning Technologies Part 2: Applications of Artificial Intelligence to Contemporary and Emerging Educational Challenges," AI Mag. 34(4), 2013, pp. 10-12.

[7] "Exclusive Interview with Donald Norman," 2001, URL:http://www.elearningpost.com/articles/archives/exclusive_interview_with_donald_norman/ [accessed: 2019-01-10].

[8] F. G. Hamza-Lup and I. R. Goldbach, "Hybrid Courses and Associated Distributed Learning Paradigms," Intl. Symp. on Computer Science and Intelligent Control, Budapest, Hungary, October, 20-22, 2017, pp. 164-166, doi: 10.1109/ISCSIC.2017.12.

[9] F. G. Hamza-Lup and S. White, "Design and Assessment for Hybrid Courses: Insights and Overviews," Intl. Journal of Advances in Life Sciences, Vol. 7(3), 2015, pp. 122-31.

[10] "Mobile Device Access for U.S. Students in Grades 4-12 on the Rise," Pearson Mobile Device Survey, 2015.

[11] M. Guzdial and K. Carroll, "Exploring the lack of dialogue in computer-supported collaborative learning," Proceedings of Computer Support for Collaborative Learning: Foundations for a CSCL Community, 2002, pp. 418-424.

[12] R. E. Banchs, R. Jiang, S. Kim, A. Niswar, and K. H. Yeo, "AIDA: Artificial Intelligent Dialogue Agent," Proceedings of the SIGDIAL 2013 Conference, Association for Computational Linguistics, 2013, pp 145-147.

[13] "Asynchronous Communication Types - Request and Response Sequences." URL: https://admhelp.microfocus.com/lr/en/12.60/help/WebHelp/Content/VuGen/c_Async_intro_types.htm/ [accessed: 2019-01-07].

[14] P. Greene, "Automated Essay Scoring Remains an Empty Dream," 2018, URL: https://www.forbes.com/sites/petergreene/ [accessed: 2019-01-07].

[15] "Viv Labs," URL: http://viv.ai/ [accessed: 2019-01-07].

[16] "Mika Learning Software," 2018, URL: https://www.carnegielearning.com/products/software-platform/mika-learning-software/ [accessed: 2019-01-10].

[17] "Reducing Barriers to Care for Military Personnel and Families," 2018, URL: http://ict.usc.edu/wp-content/uploads/overviews/ [accessed: 2019-01-10].

[18] "About CANVAS," 2018, URL: http://ict.usc.edu/wp-content/uploads/overviews/ [accessed: 2019-01-09].

[19] "Personal Assistant for Life Long Learning," 2018, URL: http://ict.usc.edu/wp-content/uploads/overviews/PAL3_Overview.pdf/ [accessed: 2019-01-09].

[20] "About TeachLive," 2018, URL: http://teachlive.org/about/about-teachlive/ [accessed: 2019-01-09].

[21] L. A. Dieker, C. E. Hughes, M. C. Hynes, and C. Straub, "Using simulated virtual environments to improve teacher performance," J. Nat. Assoc. for Prof. Dev. Sch.: Special Issue: Technology to Enhance PDS, 10(3), 2017, pp. 62-81.

[22] "Talk, Tutor, Explore, Learn: Intelligent Tutoring and Exploration for Robust Learning", URL: http://www.italk2learn.eu/ [accessed: 2019-01-09].

[23] B. P. Woolf, "AI and Education: Celebrating 30 Years of Marriage," AIED Workshop Proc., vol. 4, 2015, pp.38-47.

[24] F. G. Hamza-Lup and I. A. Stanescu, "The Haptic Paradigm in Education: Challenges and Case Studies," The Internet and Higher Education Journal, vol.13(1-2), Special Issue on the Community of Inquiry Framework: Ten Years Later, 2010, pp.78-81, ISSN: 1096-7516.

[25] F. G. Hamza-Lup and I. Sopin, "Web-Based 3D and Haptic Interactive Environments for e-Learning, Simulation, and Training," In J. Cordeiro, S. Hammoudi and J. Filipe (Eds.), Web Info. Sys. and Technologies, Berlin: Springer Berlin Heidelberg, 2009, pp. 349-360, ISBN 978-3-642-01343-0.

Recommendation Acceptance in a Simple Adaptive Learning System

Matthias Holthaus, Tansu Pancar, Per Bergamin
UNESCO chair on personalized and adaptive distance education
Swiss Distance University of Applied Sciences (FFHS)
Brig, Switzerland

Email: matthias.holthaus@ffhs.ch, tansu.pancar@ffhs.ch, per.bergamin@ffhs.ch

Abstract - **In the following article we report the current status of our research on integrating a simple, useful adaptive learning system into a university's standard learning management system. In this context, a corresponding instructional design was implemented for a basic mathematics course with the aim of supporting students in their self-study. A rule-based tool was developed for this purpose. The theoretical basis of the design was the Cognitive Load Theory. Based on the principles of this theory, the load on the working memory of the students during learning was to be optimized by appropriate task difficulties. It was expected that the learning performance would be improved. The first results from one of our preliminary studies focusing on learning progress, activity and previous knowledge of different groups of students showed that students who actively worked with adaptive tasks benefited from the system and achieved a greater learning progress than the comparison groups. In the follow-up to this finding, new research questions have arisen for us on the basis of certain limits of the previous study. All of these questions aim to determine whether the positive learning effects can be attributed to the increase in learning activities alone or to following the recommendations or to the interaction of both. In this paper, we present the next research steps in the sense of a framework in order to find the corresponding answers.**

Keywords - technology-based learning; adaptive learning; recommendation system; cognitive load; learning management system; log files.

I. INTRODUCTION

Many areas of our society and social life are increasingly subject to digitalization. This also applies to the area of education and learning. Accordingly, new forms of learning are emerging and gaining importance, such as distance or blended learning concepts or also pure technology-based learning offers. These forms of learning can be distinguished from traditional ones by their flexible characteristics [2]. For example, they enable certain forms of freedom and autonomy, they help to overcome space-time barriers, they open up new opportunities for lifelong learning, or they allow students to complete academic studies even while in full or part-time employment or parenthood. In addition, this flexibility also opens up the opportunity of individualizing or, even more, of personalizing learning on the basis of the heterogeneous characteristics or needs of learners by adapting teaching concepts, curricula, learning contents or tasks to the specific needs of the individuals. In many current training programs, specifically in higher education, it is generally expected that all learners develop the same competences, despite different prerequisites, such as pre-knowledge, learning skills, interests, motivation, social status, life situation, and so on. In addition, the learners in traditional learning offers are given the same or almost no different learning paths or learning support. In contrast to the corresponding traditional "one-size-fits-all" concept, one effective method of achieving learning success is to continuously adapt learning arrangements to the individual needs of students. The importance of adapting learning processes to the individual needs of learners is demonstrated, for example, by a phenomenon known in research on cognitive instruction design as the Expertise Reversal Effect [7][9]. It is shown that, among other things, instructions or specific assistance, which are important for beginners, lose their effect for experts or can even hinder them in their learning. From a technological point of view, adaptive learning environments or adaptive arrangements can be provided within a learning environment by a more or less complex Learning Management System (LMS).

Today, studies on adaptive learning concepts are becoming increasingly common, but practical implementations are still scarce [6][16]. Price et al. [14] argue that there is a gap between research and practice that appears to be systemic in nature and requires change at several levels, including institutional change. FitzGerald et al. [3] in contrast assume that individualization in technology-based learning can be seen as positive and promising, but that its implementation is difficult to realize. While some, such as Murray and Pérez [13], assume that the cause is more to be found in technology-based learning environments, they look to the educational sciences and less to the technological side to drive forward a corresponding transformation. However, in order to bridge the gap between research and practice, we need an interdisciplinary approach with broad-based field studies in appropriate contexts and the further development of sound didactic concepts [15]. In one of our own studies [5] we show, for instance, that a viable adaptive concept for a basic mathematics course (university level) can be realized in a simple way via a standard learning management system (Moodle) using a blended learning scenario during a whole semester. In particular, novices with low pre-knowledge and high learning activity benefit from this concept regarding their learning progress.

On the basis of these results, the present study aims to answer a further question, which has not yet been assessed: whether the positive learning effects found in the preliminary study are attributable to the increase in learning activities or rather to recommendations of the learning system. In the following, the adaptive learning system developed by us is described and the results of the preliminary study are summarized. We then discuss the further research questions and methodological approaches (data collection and evaluation) arising from the limitations of the preliminary study.

II. Implementation and First exploratory Findings

A. Implementation of the Adaptive Learning System and Instruction Design based on the Cognitive Load Theory

The above-mentioned adaptive learning concept was developed and implemented as part of a degree program for business engineers. For this purpose, we implemented 84 adaptive online tasks and made them available to the students for the autumn semester 2017/18 through the learning platform. The blended learning scenario consisted of 20% learning time as a face-to-face sessions and 80% as self-study. This included literature study on the one hand and the possibility to acquire required skills by intensive practicing with interactive tasks (in this case in adaptive form) on the other hand. The adaptive tasks themselves covered all learning objectives of the course.

Various authors (e.g. [11]) propose a learner model on a theoretical basis for the development of adaptive learning environments. In this context, we focused more on a basic theory of information processing the Cognitive Load Theory [17] as a framework. In this theoretical approach, it is assumed that the working memory has only a limited capacity. Three types of cognitive loads influence its information processing processes. The intrinsic cognitive load (1) arises from the actual learning content respectively from the number of information connections of a learning task. The extraneous cognitive load (2) results from demands outside a learning task and is caused, for example, by the presentation of the learning material or by the teachers themselves. This form of load is increased by unfavorable instructional methods, e.g., by distracting information or unnecessary complexity of a task. The germane cognitive load (3) results from the development of new or the extension of existing cognitive schemata which are stored in the long-term memory. It is regarded as desirable, since new information is built up or the basis for new skills is laid in this context.

Generally, the theory of cognitive load can be applied to any learning context (e.g., offline or online). To improve learning, it is assumed that the intrinsic load should be optimized, supporting measures to promote introduction of germane load and/or minimize extraneous load.

In the present study, we focused especially on the individually adapted improvement of the learning situation with regard to the intrinsic load and the associated extrinsic load [8][10]. Therefore, the difficulty and design of tasks in learning processes were to be planned and regulated in such a way that many resources in the working memory could be kept free for the germane cognitive load and therefore for information processing. Utilizing these assumptions, we designed an adaptive learning process in which learners with low pre-knowledge or low learning performance received much support and guidance when solving mathematical learning tasks so that they were not overburdened by the complexity of the new learning content and information. In contrast, learners with a high level of pre-knowledge or high learning performance received little help and guidance, as superfluous support would disturb them and possibly even impede learning (see the Expertise Reversal Effect [7, 9]). Consequently, mathematical tasks were developed using these learning designs. Each task contained the same mathematical problem and learning goals, but differed in the quantity and type of solution steps and provided different levels of detail or assistance in the case of insufficient performance.

Based on a model by Zimmermann et al. [18], we used three resources to implement the adaptation. These served to continuously measure the characteristics of the learners and the current learning behavior (in the present context learning performance), to compare the measurements with the desired target values, and then, in case of discrepancies, to initiate teaching reactions with the assistance mentioned above. As a first source, results of pre-knowledge tests with which students started their online course activities were used. Depending on the result, the students automatically received feedback on their current knowledge and their classification in our system as "high" performer or "low" performer. Accordingly, they received either detailed tasks with many intermediate steps and much support when classified as low performer or non-detailed tasks with little support for the high performers (see also Figure 1). The second source of adaptation was the solution behavior of the students. The tasks were divided into individual steps or questions depending on performance. When the student answered a question, he immediately received corresponding feedback. In the event of incorrect answers, the student received up to three different types of assistance. The immediate feedback and the corresponding solutions were meant to rapidly close and/or avoid knowledge gaps. The third source of adaptation could be found between the tasks. After each standard task, a transfer task was recommended to the students in order to work on the respective learning objective again. This horizontal learning transfer was supposed to help to test and to stabilize the knowledge. Transfer tasks were similar to standard tasks. They dealt with a similar or slightly different problems than the standard tasks and could be solved with mathematical methods already learned. Depending on their performance, low performers were recommended to perform the detailed standard task again or a non-detailed transfer task, while high performers were suggested to perform either the detailed standard task or a non-detailed transfer task. Under certain circumstances, high performers may also have received a suggestion to proceed to a new task set. In the other cases, however, this only happened with good performance in the transfer tasks. The various adaptive learning paths are shown in an overview in Figure 1. For a more detailed description of the learning system see [5].

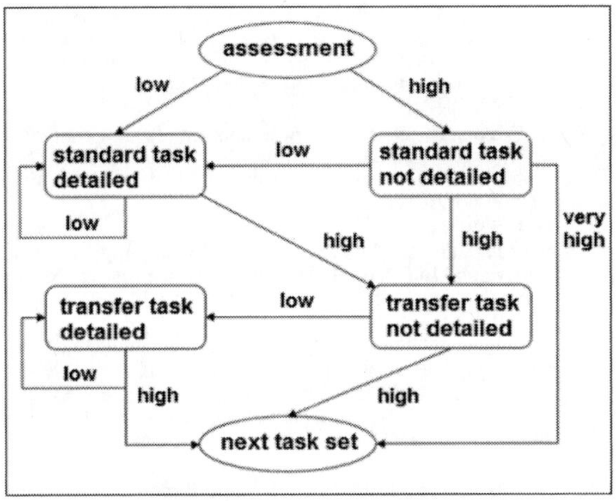

Figure 1. Task Set for a Learning Goal

The entire adaptive system was based on recommendations. Students could follow them or decide not to. Thus, the intention was that the students have to make their own learning decisions, which in turn helped to assess their own learning. The recommendations were guided by a pre-defined set of rules. Defined threshold values for the number of points achieved defined which task was recommended next (see also Figure 1 and for more details [5]).

The entire adaptive learning system was based on a standard Learning Management System (Moodle) without additional plugin. It worked with the conditions/restrictions that were available in the core of Moodle (from version 3.3+ on). A specific advantage of this variant without plugin was a guaranteed stability. Using plugins often lead to problems and revisions due to possible compatibility problems between core and plugin when updating.

B. Current Findings and new Research Questions

In a first explorative analysis [5] of the adaptive concept for a basic mathematics course, we focused on possible performance improvements of students by investigating the relationship between three variables: pre-knowledge (in other words low performer and high performer), online activity (log files), and learning progress. It turned out that students working actively online in the adaptive course achieved significantly better learning progress than the students who did not. The learning progress was defined as the difference between the results of the prior knowledge test, standardized to 100, and the results of the final examination, also standardized to 100. The average learning progress of the "inactive" students was 8.4, that of the "active" ones 32.4 (the difference is significant, verified by a t-test, $p < 0.05$).

In addition, the analysis showed that the active low performers in an adaptive version of the course showed significantly higher learning progress compared to all low performers in a non-adaptive variant of the same course (mean value of active low performer in the adaptive course: 49.2, mean value of all low performer non-adaptive course: 19.0; tested by a one-sided ANOVA with Tamhane post hoc test, $p = 0.01$).

A comparable result with a significant difference was also found when comparing active high performer of the adaptive course with all high performer of the non-adaptive version (mean value of active high performer in the adaptive course: 22.2, mean value of all high performer in the non-adaptive course: -12.1, tested with a one-sided ANOVA with Tamhane post hoc test, $p = .01$, see also [5]).

On the basis of these results, it could be assumed that the adaptive teaching design, implemented in the learning platform, facilitated the learning progress of active online students compared to a non-adaptive design. However, the analysis was limited in that it was not clear whether the improved learning progress was only due to the increased activity or to the enhancement of learning processes through the optimization of cognitive load (assumption in our design) by following the recommendations of the adaptive system.

In order to clarify this question and to continue the work, we therefore formulated the following four research questions for further investigation.

a. How do the students follow the recommendations?
b. Which parameters best predict the following subsequences (Logs) of the recommendations?
c. Which groups follow the recommendations more?
d. How does following the recommendations affect the learning behavior?

In order to be able to answer these questions, we need a complete tracking of the online activities of the students as well as information on the self-monitoring of the students of their own learning activities. With the current work, we also want to check which recommendations are more likely to be accepted by students and which are not, and in this way modify and improve the recommendation system if necessary.

III. Work in Progress

A. Collecting Data

For further investigation and to answer the research questions, we use self-declaration by the students by evaluating their own mathematical knowledge (by asking short questions at the beginning of the course and storing the answers in the database of the learning platform) and also by individual log files or entire sequences of log files with time stamp. Each online action of a user is tracked and registered in a database in the following form: Time stamp of the action, personal identification of the user and event name.

This creates sequences of log files that can indicate what the user has done in what time. This also means that it is possible to track which tasks (steps) were processed at which time in which action sequence, trial amount and also results (e.g., right/wrong). It is also possible to check on the basis of the log file sequences whether the tasks were processed according to the rule based recommendations (see Figure 1) or whether the users performed other online actions in between. In addition, it is also possible to estimate how much time elapsed between the recommendations and the subsequent actions.

With the above data, we will test and validate three methodological assessment procedures to obtain an indicator of "how students follow the recommendations":

1. In the first procedure, we consider only the next entry in the database that follows the recommendation. So, we check whether students go directly to the next recommended task without doing another online activity first. We assume that the students who directly execute the system's recommendations are less self-monitoring in their own learning. The index is calculated as the percentage of recommendations followed.
2. The second method is to look at a sequence of log files after the student has received a recommendation. This involves observing when students follow recommendations and how much online activity they perform before they follow a recommendation [1][4][12]. We assume that these students monitor their own learning behavior more closely and accept a recommendation accordingly or do not follow it after consideration. For this purpose, we want to measure the average number of logs until the student starts the recommended online activity.
3. In the third procedure, as an alternative to the two previous methods, we will use, for students who followed a recommendation, the average time until the student starts a corresponding online activity after a recommendation as an index.

B. Data evaluation

For the first two procedures, we will test the predictive validity and for the third method, we will check whether integration of "time" as an additional parameter results in a better predictive power.

With a focus on all above mentioned research questions, we intend to combine the data resulting from the above-mentioned methods with different groups of students. One criterion for the differentiation of students is their self-evaluated mathematical knowledge at the beginning of their studies. It is then analyzed whether different evaluations have an influence on the acceptance of the system's recommendations. A further goal is to determine how different prior knowledge (measured by the standard mathematical test of the adaptive system) influences the following of recommendations. The same relationships are also explored for the frequency and type (self-monitoring) of online activities (recorded by logs) and learning performance (progress and performance in the final test).

The results of the study should be available by the end of 2019 and published subsequently.

REFERENCES

[1] A. Abbott, “Sequence Analysis: New Methods for old Ideas,” Annual Review of Sociology, 21(1), pp. 93-113, 1995. https://doi: 10.1146/annurev.so.21.080195.000521

[2] P. Bergamin, E. Werlen, E. Siegenthaler, and S. Ziska, "The Relationship between Flexible and Self-Regulated Learning in Open and Distance Universities," International Review of Research in Open and Distance Learning, vol. 13, no. 2, pp. 101–123, 2012.

[3] E. FitzGerald et al., "Dimensions of Personalisation in Technologyenhanced Learning: A Framework and Implications for Design," British Journal of Educational Technology, 2017. https://doi.org/10.1111/bjet.12534

[4] A. Gabadinho, G. Ritschard, N. S. Mueller, and M. Studer, "Analyzing and Visualizing State Sequences in R with TraMineR," Journal of Statistical Software, 40(4), pp. 1-37, 2011.

[5] M. Holthaus, F. Hirt, and P. Bergamin, "Simple and Effective: An Adaptive Instructional Design for Mathematics Implemented in a Standard Learning Management System," CHIRA 2018 - 2nd International Conference on Computer-Human Interaction Research and Applications - Proceedings, pp. 116 - 126, 2018.

[6] L. Johnson et al., "NMC Horizon Report: 2016 Higher Education Edition." Austin, Texas: The New Media Consortium, 2016.

[7] S. Kalyuga, "Expertise Reversal Effect and Its Implications for Learner-Tailored Instruction," Educational Psychology Review, 19(4), pp.509–539, 2007.

[8] S. Kalyuga, "Cognitive Load Theory: How Many Types of Load Does It Really Need," Educational Psychology Review, 23(1), pp. 1-19, 2011. https://doi.org/10.1007/s10648-010-9150-7

[9] S. Kalyuga, P. Ayres, P. Chandler, and J. Sweller, "The Expertise Reversal Effect," Educational Psychologist, 38(1), pp.23–3, 2003.

[10] S. Kalyuga and A.-M. Singh, "Rethinking the Boundaries of Cognitive Load Theory in Complex Learning," Educational Psychology Review, 28(4), pp. 831-852, 2016.

[11] C. Limongelli, F. Sciarrone, M. Temperini, and G. Vaste, “Adaptive Learning with the LS-PLAN System: a Field Evaluation,” IEEE Transactions on Learning Technologies, 2(3), pp. 203-215, 2009.

[12] Z. Liu, H. Dev, M. Dontcheva, and M. Hoffman, "Mining, Pruning and Visualizing Frequent Patterns for Temporal Event Sequence Analysis," Proceedings of the IEEE VIS 2016 Workshop on Temporal & Sequential Event Analysis, 2016. http://eventevent.github.io

[13] M. C. Murray and J. Pérez, "Informing and Performing: A Study Comparing Adaptive Learning to Traditional Learning," Informing Science, 18(1), pp.111–125, 2015.

[14] L. Price, D. Casanova, and S. Orwell, "Modeling an Institutional Approach to Developing Technology Enabled Learning: Closing the Gap between Research and Practice," INTED2017 Proceedings, pp.5009–5018, 2017.

[15] E. Scanlon, T. O’Shea, and P. McAndrew, "Technology-Enhanced Learning: Evidence-based Improvement," L@S ’15 Proceedings of the Second (2015) ACM Conference on

Learning @ Scale." Vancouver, BC, Canada: ACM New York, NY, USA, pp. 229–232, 2015.

[16] S. Somyürek, "The New Trends in Adaptive Educational Hypermedia Systems," International Review of Research in Open and Distributed Learning, 16(1), pp.221–241, 2015.

[17] J. Sweller, "Cognitive Load During Problem Solving: Effects on Learning, "Cognitive Science, 12(2), pp. 257-285, 1988.

[18] A. Zimmermann, M. Specht, and A. Lorenz, "Personalization and Context Management," User Modeling and User-Adapted Interaction, 15(3), pp. 275-302, 2005.